Zen and the Art of Business Communication

Zen and the Art of Business Communication

A Step-by-Step Guide to Improving Your Business Writing Skills

Susan L. Luck, PhD

BUSINESS EXPERT PRESS

Zen and the Art of Business Communication: A Step-by-Step Guide to Improving Your Business Writing Skills
Copyright © Business Expert Press, LLC, 2016

First published in 2016 by
Business Expert Press, LLC
222 East 46th Street, New York, NY 10017
www.businessexpertpress.com

ISBN-13: 978-1-60649-956-6 (paperback)
ISBN-13: 978-1-60649-957-3 (e-book)

Business Expert Press Corporate Communication Collection

Collection ISSN: 2156-8162 (print)
Collection ISSN: 2156-8170 (electronic)

Cover and interior design by S4Carlisle Publishing Services
Private Ltd., Chennai, India
Illustrations Credit by Celia Luck-Leonard

First edition: 2016

10 9 8 7 6 5 4 3 2 1

Printed in the United States of America.

Dedication

To my family.

Abstract

In today's online world, our professional image depends on our ability to communicate. Whether we're communicating by email, text, social media, written reports, or presentations, how we use our words often determines how others view us. This book offers tips and techniques that can improve anyone's professional image. It covers how to analyze your multiple audiences and strategies for communicating your message effectively for each; structuring your message for greatest readability and effect; persuasion and tone; and how to face your own fears of writing. The content is delivered in a simple, clear style that reflects the Zen approach of the title, perfect for both the entry-level employee and the seasoned executive.

Key words

business communication; managerial communication; business writing; managerial writing; organizational communication; leadership communication; good writing; writing advice; grammar for business; writing for business; professional image

Contents

Acknowledgments

I'd like to acknowledge all the people who have helped make this book possible, from the students who needed me to explain theory in a straight-forward manner to those of my friends and colleagues who encouraged me to write those explanations down. I'd also like to thank Debbie DuFrene, who took a chance on my idea; my daughter Celia Luck-Leonard who said the book needed illustrations; and Premkumar Narayanan, who had infinite patience with me while putting the book together.

CHAPTER 1

Introduction

Either write something worth reading or do something worth writing.
—Benjamin Franklin

Why does writing matter? Well, for one, as our world becomes increasingly digitalized, your written image is your public image. By that I mean most of the people you do business with, connect with, or even sit in class with don't see you in person. They see you in your words—their first, and sometimes only, impression of you comes from what you write.

That written image can come from email, text or instant messaging, or even in a blog post or comments. It can be the replies you give to questions your employees ask. It can be your written reports—or the writing that you do for a PowerPoint presentation you upload online. No matter what it is, it becomes you. What you look like, sound like, and act like doesn't matter. The only things that matter are your words and how you use them.

Even your social media is written communication. Not only can your friends and followers see what you have tweeted or posted on Facebook; potential employers as well as your current employers also can, no matter how many privacy settings you put on. Yes, often these employers are checking to make sure you don't slander the company or make bomb threats, but they are also checking to see how well you communicate in written form. Your competitors also are taking note.

Nothing gives a person an edge better than being a clearer and more correct writer.

How does good writing make you competitive? Well, let's start with the results of the 2011 National Assessment Governing Board's Nation's Report Card tests: in 2011, fewer than 24% of all American high school seniors were considered proficient in writing at a 12th grade level. That was a 9% drop from 2007—and an additional 5% drop from the 2001 test. The College Board, those folks who put out the SAT, reported that in 2009 American businesses had to spend over $3.1 billion on remedial writing skills for their college-graduate employees—and yes, that isn't a typo; that is indeed $3.1 billion.

Furthermore, a 2007 report by *Esquire* editor A.J. Jacobs stated that companies could hire someone in India or China for $4.35 an hour who could write in English better than most U.S. college graduates between the ages of 23 and 35. And we wonder why outsourcing is still alive and well.

So what is one to do? We could sit and wring our hands, moaning about how we were shortchanged in school. Or we could employ that old American adage: stop complaining, put on our grown-up clothes, and do something about the situation. And doing something doesn't have to be hard. It can be step-by-step and logical. It can be simple. In fact, it can even be enjoyable. That's where the Zen comes in.

So What's Zen?

Zen is a form of Buddhism that emerged in 6th century China. It's a very accepting and calm spiritual practice, espousing that all people are born enlightened but have allowed the hustle and chaos of the world to cloud that enlightenment with ignorance. According to Zen, ignorance comes from never having been taught or exposed to something, which is a perfectly acceptable reason for being ignorant. It also teaches that we can fall into ignorance by believing falsehoods that we have gathered from all the noise of the world around us. To overcome this clouded thinking, we have to face reality and accept facts and life as they are, examine them, and use the simplest approach to overcome or accept them.

Buddha is thought to have used a form of Zen to reach a sudden enlightenment. Zen has no deities to worship, no sacred texts to study, and no real obligations other than simplicity and mindfulness. The promise of Zen is that if we practice simplicity and mindfulness, we will find enlightenment in ourselves again.

Zen is not a religion. Zen is a method, an approach toward life. It's a way to overcome the chaos in our lives. Practicing a Zen approach to business communication can help us control all the unseen zingers coming at us. The practice also gives us the ability to find time for ourselves and for enjoying life, as well as finding that we do our best work and are our best selves in the process.

In other words, using simplicity and mindfulness can allow us to overcome our inner gerbil. My kids used to have two gerbils; they were classroom pets that we "won" in an end-of-the-year raffle where the kindergartners got to vie to see who would be the lucky ones to inherit them when the school year was over. (We also won a guinea pig that way, but that is another story.) Inside their cage was an exercise wheel. About 20 times a day, one of the gerbils would get on that wheel and run hell-bent for leather, as fast as he could go, for as long as he could go, until he got dizzy, fell off the wheel, and collapsed for a few minutes at the bottom of the cage.

That gerbil symbolized how most of us run our work lives. And although the cage he lived in was pretty palatial as far as gerbil cages go, with two stories, several toys, and fresh and varied food three times a day, he still lived in a cage. One of the beauties of a Zen approach to a work life is that instead of running like crazy to get nowhere, we proceed with deliberation. True, we have to have an eye on the destination and an eye on the future, but by being immensely aware of the present, we enjoy the trip. By being in the moment, we do a much better job—and as a result, we create a better future.

The other gerbil, by the way, would get on the wheel once or twice a day. He would run at a steady pace, last longer at it than his counterpart, and when done would step confidently off the wheel and mosey over to the food bowl. He was the gerbil who interacted with us more, who was more aware of the movement and people outside the cage, and who would try new foods that we would put in the cage. He also seemed comfortable being out of the cage, allowing people to hold him. And he loved getting in his rolling ball and letting it take him all over the kitchen. (His cage mate wouldn't even let us put him in the ball.)

"So what?" you may be thinking. "I'm not a gerbil." OK, you're not. But Zen teaches us that every living thing has something in common, and most of us are running on that gerbil wheel more than we care to admit. If we want to control the wheel rather than have it control us, we need a different approach. So if we accept that almost all of our work lives—indeed, all of our lives period—depend in some fashion on communication, and that the evidence indicates that most of us aren't very good at communication, the simplest answer is that by fixing our communication, we can improve our work lives and our careers.

The question is *how.*

The Zen of Good Communications

The philosophy of Zen Buddhism emphasizes experiential wisdom in the attainment of enlightenment. As such, it de-emphasizes theoretical knowledge in favor of direct self-realization. Once devotees have that realization, they focus on it. They ponder and apply it, then watch the results. By doing so, they stay present in the moment. They take the time to see the details and experience them, which in turn simplifies the realization. Through use of the simplicity, they approach wisdom.

Hard work? Maybe. You don't have to start from scratch each time, however. You can take someone else's realization, ponder it, and then apply it for your own enlightenment. That's what this book intends to do: provide you with the concept. Your job is to explore the details, apply them, and practice them. Ready?

> Here is the Zen concept that successful business writers practice: communication isn't about you.

As life becomes more and more hectic, and as we rely more and more on electronic communication, we lose the realization that communication isn't about getting the task off our plate. It isn't about barking orders to our family and employees. It isn't about the message. It's about how the receiver of the communication receives the message.

Note the Pronoun: I

When we think in "I" terms—first-person terms—we narrow our communication to our own experience and needs. We therefore miss sending any relevant information that the receiver may want. But if we eliminate the word "I" and think instead *"Helen needs to know about the meeting tomorrow"* or *"Alan needs this report by Friday,"* something interesting happens in our brains: our focus becomes more specific as well as broader.

By taking the "I" out, we think of the receiver, which in turn allows us to see things from the receiver's point of view. We suddenly are aware of more details that the receiver needs to know. We suddenly see a larger scope for the communication and why it exists at all. We even see that what makes sense in our minds is totally unclear to someone else. So we fix our communication drastically without even being aware that we have done so—all from changing the way we say the idea to ourselves.

> A good writer does 90 percent of the work so that the reader has to do only 10 percent.

Think in terms of the receiver. You will find that your self-realization improves considerably, and that your employees, colleagues, and family members will thank you. The ancient Buddhists believed that one should take at least two years to practice a concept before one could say one had realized the concept. But with each step of the practice, you are closer to the ideal; one step at a time, my friend. And with each step, you get better.

How This Book Is Focused

Although you will notice that most of the concepts that this book discusses are explained in terms of writing, the basic principles apply to all forms of business communication. Your verbal communication will also benefit from these lessons, whether **you** are giving a formal presentation or just speaking to your boss. Your video conferences will have more sophistication. And those PowerPoint presentations will be easy to follow.

How? Through simplicity.

So many business people want to present a professional image to those they work with and for. Yet they don't have all the tools to do so, especially in communication. Usually what I hear from them is that they want to sound intelligent and capable. So they revert to the only point of reference they know: the SAT words.

Many of us remember memorizing an enormous number of vocabulary words that we were told would be on the SAT, that wonderful standardized test would determine whether we got into college. (The SAT wasn't the only factor in our admission, but that's another story.) So somehow we associated these words—which were usually words that we didn't hear all that much, and that often had more than two syllables—with the idea of *smart person*. We need to know these words to get into college; smart people go to college; therefore, if we want people to know we are smart, we should use these words. Because most of us had a very basic, if any, introduction to logic, we never questioned whether that conclusion was indeed accurate.

As a result, we wound up using big words just to use big words. We hear junk such as "The perpetrator of the misdemeanor was apprehended while absconding with a motorized vehicle in a public place of recreation" instead of "The suspect was caught while stealing a car in the park." By the way, this misconception about big words isn't new or a result of cell phones or whatever we want to blame. During World War II, as writing mythology tells us, the U.S. government issued the following directive:

> *Such preparations shall be made as will completely obscure all Federal buildings and non-Federal buildings occupied by the Federal government during an air raid for any period of time from visibility by reason of internal or external illumination.*

As the story goes, when workers couldn't agree on what the memo meant, Franklin Roosevelt, who was president at the time, read it and translated for his aides, "Tell them, that in buildings where they have to keep the world going, to put something across the windows."

More recently, in July 2014, Microsoft CEO Satya Nadella issued a 3,000 word memo that had four parts and was so obtuse that high-ranking editors from the *Wall Street Journal* and the *New York Times*—no slouches when it comes to deciphering messages—could find only one thing that the memo conveyed: big changes were coming to Microsoft. Whether those changes meant that prices or products were changing, big executives were on the way out, or whether Microsoft itself was heading to the business graveyard was unclear.

Quartz writer Jean-Louis Glasee was a little more direct in his analysis, saying in effect that what Nadella needed was a good editor, stating that "clarity and ease were missing" from the memo and that "Satya Nadella's latest message to the troops—and to the world—is disquieting. It lacks

focus, specifics, and, if not soon sharpened, his words will worry employees, developers, customers, and even shareholders."

I'm not saying that one shouldn't ever use those SAT words. I'm not
saying that one shouldn't ever use big words. I am saying that if we use
those words—in fact, if we use any words at all—we need to know that
we have chosen exactly the right word to get our message across. As the
old Mark Twain adage goes,

"Never use a quarter word when a nickel word will do."

The British writer George Orwell would adapt this adage decades later
to "Never use a multisyllabic word when a one or two-syllable word will
do." Basically, all Orwell did was define quarter and nickel words.

Note Twain didn't say never use a quarter word. What he was trying to
get across was that big words alone will not make one sound professional
or smart. What he was saying was that sounding professional or smart
comes from precision in language, simplicity in form and structure, and a
conscious and deliberate awareness of what one is communicating.

That, my friends, is Zen.

Awareness and consciousness of the moment and of others, simplicity,
and precision are all hallmarks of Zen.

They are also hallmarks of good professional communication—and
they just happen to be the guiding focus of this book. Good communicators know just what to say and how to say it. They don't scream, bombast,
or ramble. They listen intently. They focus. They simplify even the most
difficult concept. And as a result, they are easy to be around.

Good communicators are great to work for. You will always know where
you stand and what you need to do. You will find that you relax and enjoy
your work. Even your body changes, becoming less tense and breathing
more naturally. The stress abates, and you get more done. And the beautiful
thing about being a good communicator is that you get every one of those
benefits your employees get; in fact you get them in greater abundance.

However. . . . .

Like almost everything else in life, this simplicity comes with a para-
doxical price tag. You have to work hard to reach this spot of simplicity. Like Michael Jackson's moonwalk, Michael Jordan's jump shots, and

Tom Brady's passes, these seemingly simple acts of beauty came from lots and lots of practice. They honed their crafts, learning from everyone they could. They practiced, adapted, and absorbed the concepts and nuances until they were that moonwalk or jump shot. Remember the old movie *Caddyshack* where Chevy Chase told Michael O'Keefe that to be great at golf he had to be the ball?

But they didn't just show up one day and poof!—they had the moonwalk, pass, and jump shot down pat. Brady was drafted in the sixth round, deemed not valuable to lead an NFL team. He was the Patriots' fourth string quarterback, during which time he waited, watched, and prepared. He went beyond the usual training camp regimen, bulking up and working on his throws. By doing so, he became one of the winningest quarterbacks in NFL history.

Jordan didn't make his high school basketball team. And when he wasn't selected, he didn't make excuses and go off and pout. Instead, he analyzed what he needed to do to be good enough to play. He broke down each item into small manageable areas to practice and then sought out coaching and advice to find ways to improve. He practiced. He didn't expect miracles. But when he showed up at UNC to play for Dean Smith, miracles occurred. Why? He worked on his game, shot by shot, step by step.

And that's what this book will offer you: small steps that, when practiced and used and absorbed, will build on each other to lead to something good. I'm not promising miracles. But I am promising that people will notice that you communicate better than you did. And I am promising that you will feel better about your communication skills. That will in turn lead to your projecting what you set out to have in the first place: the image of a professional and smart person.

Hint: If you find yourself saying "I have to do this" and approaching the techniques the way you'd approach a root canal, back off. Breathe. In fact, breathe for about three minutes—just breathe. Then look around you. What do you see? Be in the moment. Find one thing around you that sparks your interest. Breathe. Then imagine how you would describe that one thing to a four-year-old.

You will have just brought yourself back from the Worry and back to Zen. Slow it down. Forcing things never works. Slow it down and enjoy the ride.

Why All This Emphasis on Writing?
I Can Talk Just Fine

Why is writing becoming increasingly important? Well, in our global technology-driven age, your writing is often your image. It's usually, unfortunately, *you*. Most people meet you via the written word long before they meet you in person; you can do business via email or LinkedIn long before you actually speak to the person at the other end of your communications.

Roughly 40 percent of all American workers spend over half their work days on a computer. Not all of that time is number crunching; and even if you do crunch numbers, you have to put the results in a report—and that report has to be written. You may have to sum up a phone call in a written record; you may just need to send information to a colleague across town or even across the room. But you still have to write.

You can wear an Armani suit, have a $100 haircut, and own the best pair of shoes money can buy, but if your writing is sloppy, demonstrates inappropriate tone, lacks clarity, and shows no understanding of the reader's perception, then you might as well be sitting at home in your underwear with a two-day-old beard.

What the reader sees on screen is his perception of you. You may not mean to sound harsh or aggressive, but perhaps your word choice has sent that message for you. The reader can't see your smile behind words that could be perceived as sarcastic or even mean—and please don't even begin to think that adding dancing smiley faces will send the right emotion for you. Those emoticons don't clarify tone; they emphasize that you could be more in control of your communications than you currently are.

Today's workplace needs good writers.

But I Never Liked English Class. Emoting on Paper
Isn't My Thing

Good writing, however, doesn't mean pouring out your soul or describing a sky in a poetic manner. Good writing, regardless of whether it's for English class, or describing the 49ers game, or presenting the results of the second quarter sales figures, exhibits the same hallmarks: crisp and clear command of the language, with no distracting vagaries or grammatical mistakes.

If you didn't like analyzing Robert Frost's poetry, you can at least recognize what made him a good writer. Go back and take a look at what techniques Frost was using to get his message across. Frost was pretty adept in summing up complex ideas in one statement, as in his famous line from "Mending Walls" that "good fences make good neighbors." He didn't go wandering around the point. He announced what he was writing about in the first line or two of his poems so the reader always knew where he was going.

In fact, Frost had in his poems the same qualities that good CEOs have in their communication: brevity, clarity, direction, and something worthwhile to say. Business writing is all about clarity and analytical thinking. (Most writing, even fiction, is all about clarity and analytical thinking; it's just packaged in different ways for different genres.) Zen is all about finding clarity and analyzing deeply. It requires focus and self-understanding. In fact, good writing has a lot more in common with math and science than most of us realize.

OK, I Will Accept That. But I Was Never a Good Writer So How Can I Be One Now?

You probably have heard that old saying that the journey of a thousand miles begins with a single step. Zen will teach you that first, single step is a change in your focus. Are you just looking at the surface, reacting from the emotion of prior experiences, as you ask that question about how you can be a good writer now? Are you letting fear stand in your way?

Here's the first step: accept that maybe right now, in this moment, you aren't the writer you would like to be. As a result, you aren't the communicator you would like to be. Zen is all about accepting right where you are now. Leave the judgment out of it. What you are as a communicator *right now* is neither good nor bad. It just is.

And it can get better. You can be terrific at writing, by the way, and still get better. When J.K. Rowling of Harry Potter fame released her fifth book, *Harry Potter and the Order of the Phoenix*, one of the early reviewers of the book was Stephen King, who is no slouch himself when it comes to writing. While he praised her work highly, saying that with that book she had left the realm of children's literature and had entered the higher world of literature itself—and had done a real bang-up job in doing so as well—she still had some problems with overwriting. Particularly, he was annoyed with the adverbs she kept putting in her attributions, as in *Harry said stubbornly* and *Hermione admitted resignedly.* Cut the adverbs, he advised, and the writing, while stellar now, will be much better.

Did Rowling sit and sulk? She did not. In fact, she contacted King to thank him for helping her become a better writer. The two developed into writing buddies who now read each other's work, offering help and encouragement.

Two of the world's best writers still need help? Yes. Zen will teach you that the entire path toward enlightenment shows one ways to improve. The key is simplicity and being able to look at all the details. Being in the moment, accepting without judgment, and being willing to break down the pieces to see the whole is not only smart thinking but analytical thinking, which in turn will lead to good writing.

Take, for example, the story of one of my former students. He had been not only his high school's valedictorian but one of the top students in Texas the year he graduated. He could knock out standardized tests as easily as he could knock out a cheese pizza with extra sauce. But he found himself in my office, angry about the C he had earned on a paper.

"What do you mean, I haven't analyzed?" All six-foot-three of him quivered with indignation. "I've given you all the facts."

"Yes," I replied. "But you haven't drawn a conclusion from those facts."

"You mean you want me to tell you *why* I think what I do?" He shook his head. "I was valedictorian of my high school class, and no one ever asked me to answer that."

What this college freshman lacked, the answer to why, was the ability to think critically. He had a head stuffed full of information, but he couldn't use that information to draw an opinion. As a result, he was about to fail out of a prestigious university.

Most of us, for instance, know that the Japanese bombed Pearl Harbor on December 7, 1941. But few of us know why the Japanese did so, why that event brought the United States into the war in Europe, how that bombing played a part in forming the strategy the United States used in the European war theater, how that bombing might have been avoided, and what that bombing did to change the socio-economic structure of the western United States for two decades.

As one of my consulting clients, a CFO of a major auditing firm, complained about his auditors, "They regurgitate endless amounts of facts. But I'm paying them to draw conclusions from those facts so that I can make decisions based on their conclusions. I want them to analyze. But they keep regurgitating those facts, because they don't know the difference between doing so and thinking."

And that lack of knowledge impacts one's writing. If you can't think, how can you write? Write intelligently, I mean—in a manner that showcases who you are as you would like to be seen. Good writing is not about just letting the words flow, especially not in business. It's about deliberate, thoughtful, and accurate critical thinking, which comes only from deep awareness of what is around us. Zen, in other words.

So how does one learn critical thinking? Is a major overhaul in curriculum required? I don'tthink so. On the first Monday my daughter was in kindergarten, she came home and told me the teacher had read them a book about the Three Little Pigs. On Tuesday the teacher read a different book about the Three Little Pigs. Ditto on Wednesday and Thursday. On Friday, I asked, "So did your teacher read you another book about the Three Little Pigs?"

"No," she said, "She made us tell her which of the books we liked best and why, and then we had to tell her how the way the author wrote the story made us choose which one we liked best. We had to show her and the class stuff in the book to prove our points. Lots of us liked different books and so we had to argue for a while about why we liked which one better."

I smiled to myself. *She's teaching critical thinking.*

So How Does Critical Thinking Affect My Writing? And Why Does It Matter in Business Communications?

Critical thinking means that you have slowed down enough to look at all aspects of a situation. You have considered all angles and all audiences. You have a reason why you are communicating—and it isn't just to get something off your plate or to complain about something.

It matters in business communication because—drum roll, please—it signals that you are a grown up. It signals a maturity of thought and a professional level of thought. It sends the message that you have thought clearly and deeply about the issue and have the evidence and authority to issue the communication you have just sent out. Remember the professional image many people want to give out by using big words? Critical thinking, which then results in clear and simple writing, will earn you that image.

Breathe. Think. Look at all aspects and details. Consider. And then write. That's the path of Zen.

Ok, I'm Sold. How Do I Get Started?

Read on.

CHAPTER 2

Honor Focus

By prevailing over all obstacles and distractions, one may unfailingly arrive at his chosen goal or destination.

—Christopher Columbus

The word *focus* is bantered about our society these days as if it were something disposable: we have focus groups, we have clichés such as *getting a clear focus on whatever*, and we tell ourselves we have to focus. But do we really understand what we mean by that word?

For most of us, life is a series of interruptions. You can't go into a grocery store without hearing music in the background—and it's not the elevator soothing music of 20 years ago anymore; it's the latest pop hit interspersed with ads for the store and for other products, and it's a lot louder than it used to be. You also have in the background the myriad of conversations that people are having on their cell phones, that, try as you might, you can't totally ignore; why did that woman have to tell her son not to come over for dinner even though she was in the grocery store and why did that man tell whomever he was talking to that he was about to do something drastic at his job and furthermore, just how drastic was it, and do you need to alert the authorities?

We may find that we can't work in our offices; today's communal cubicles, in which several desks are pointed at each other, all separated by a waist-high wall intended to make the employees feel like a team, in fact force the inhabitants to hear and in some way process each other's work and conversations as well as our own. To combat that noise, we may wear headphones, which in themselves pipe music into our ears that may also distract us.

Add to that the instant messaging that shows up on our computers, the *ping!* that announces that we have at least 62 new emails, and all the coworkers who show up to stand behind you or in your office door and ask, "Got a minute?" when you clearly are working on something—you have recipe for Office ADD.

Remember the dogs in the Pixar movie *Up*? They were a lean, mean fighting machine of a pack—until a squirrel went by. Then all their attention went zooming to that squirrel, forgetting everything else. That's us—a whole battalion of worker bees responding to a constant chorus of "*squirrel!*"

So no matter how much we talk about finding focus, we have very little of it in our lives—yet it is crucial for successful Zen communication.

What Is Focus?

Many of us do our daily jobs with only the information as to how what we do affects our immediate coworkers. If we work in a large, 5000 + employee company, we may not even work in the same city, much less the same facility, where people in other departments of our companies work. As a result, we know only what we see and what is close around us.

But the problem with this situation is that by being this small isolated cog in the giant corporate wheel we lose the bigger picture of where we are doing it. The great 19th century poet Thomas Hardy talked about *"the hawk's eye view,"* which in essence meant being able to scan the entire landscape of what was before us, take in all the details, and go unerringly right to what needed to be done. That's focus.

Focus means to be able to discern the distractions and discard them, seeing what is asked from us or what we are asking of ourselves. In Zen, it is known as *mindfulness*.

Mindfulness means being able to act, not react. What does that mean? When we have thought about all the aspects of a situation, all that it is calling on us to do, and all that we intend to do in and with situation, we act. But when we just start out, without consideration of whether it is the best direction to go in, that's reaction. We react when we act out of emotion; while many people think of *reacting* as coming from anger, reacting can also come from being too overwhelmed to think through the situation.

Why Do I Need to Focus?

Of course, one of the usual reactions to the previous statement is "What do you mean, reacting? I am just getting through my day. Time is of the essence, and part of my evaluation is based on my productivity."

True. But merely being busy doesn't mean being productive. Have you ever seen an old pinball machine? The kind where you pulled a lever and then watched a ball bounce off various roadblocks, flipping more levers to steer the ball back around more roadblocks, hoping that you could hit them all before the ball sank down into the bowels of the machine and you had to start over? That's how most of us approach productivity: we are the ball in the pinball machine. We get up a huge head of steam and bounce from project to project, sometimes being sent back to hit the same project repeatedly until we sink and go home for the day—or quit working, because many of us take our work home with us once we've put in our eight or nine hours at the office.

Like the pinball, we react, rather than follow a strict direction. If you studied the pinball board, you could figure out that the best strategy for gaining the most points was in a certain pattern (each one varied

depending on the machine and how it was set up) and hitting each road-block in a certain sequence that would guarantee you the best points. Pinball wizards had the focus to be able to plan that strategy; they could see all the moves that would allow them to score.

Chess masters have that same focus. So do great quarterbacks: they have to see the holes in the players on the field and be able to think three steps ahead. Yet while chess masters usually plan in a hushed room, think about the hoopla and noise that goes on at any college or NFL football game. Those quarterbacks have to be deaf and blind to outside distractions; they have to focus. And the pinball wizards? Well, the 1960s band The Who wrote a whole rock opera about one. Called *Tommy*, the main character, who happens to be that pinball wizard, is deaf, dumb, and blind, which is the reason he's so good. Rather symbolic, isn't it?

> For communicators, focusing means to be aware of what the whole strategy behind a piece of communication, as well as aware of all the intentions and results one wants from it. Focus also means to shut out other things, such as the voices in our heads.

Most of us have running commentaries going on in our heads, much like having three different TVs on at once: *finish this quickly you have a meeting in fifteen minutes and—oh, heavens, did I sign Julie up for basketball? And when is that list for Sam due again?—and let's see, I was saying that the analysis of the data showed—what exactly did it show? I had a great way of summing that up a minute ago*—James Joyce and William James called this running commentary **stream of consciousness**, and while it is a nifty literary technique, it is also the surest way to ensure that you are the ball in the pinball machine rather than the wizard.

Lewis Carroll, best known as the author of *Alice in Wonderland*, was a brilliant mathematician and commentator on the society he saw around him. He was undoubtedly referring to observed futility when he has the Red Queen—surely the prototype of an unreasonable executive—tell Alice, "My dear, here we must run as fast as we can, just to stay in place. And if you wish to go anywhere you must run twice as fast as that." Words from a woman crazy enough to have the white roses painted red are not words that we embrace in Zen.

You have probably heard the phrase "work smarter, not harder." The problem then becomes that we don't know how to be smarter. We've

worked so hard just to stay in one place that we can't focus. We think we are faced with either staying in the race to nowhere or what appears to be the only other choice, which is drop out completely. But that is a false assumption appearing real. No matter what it seems to be, it's still false.

Why do we teach kids to "Stop, Drop, and Roll" when they see fire? Why do we tell people to think "ABC" (*airway, breathing, and circulation*) when teaching first aid? These are the first steps, yes, but they don't handle the crisis. What they do is allow us to stop running as fast as we can and be able to *think*. Thinking isn't allowing any old random thought to float through our heads. Good thinking involves focus. If we want to be productive, not have to redo our work to make it right, and make sure what we send out is the best representation of ourselves, we need to focus.

How Do I Focus?

The first step in gaining focus is the usual first step in anything Zen: breathe. Take 30 seconds—that's all you need—and just breathe. Put yourself back in the present moment, not in projection of what will happen or needs to happen in the future. Just breathe.

Now take another 30 seconds to move your thoughts from a point in front of you to a horizontal view. You can actually tell physically if you are doing so; if you find yourself staring straight ahead, with almost no peripheral details in your mind, you are not focusing. You may think that you are looking at a point in front of you, but you aren't; that point in front of you is the goal, not the focus. (We'll discuss the goal and how it is different from the focus in the next chapter.)

Breathe and pull back your visual focus from the point in front of you so that you can see the details to the side. Think of a movie camera shot: when it opens up wide, you as the viewer suddenly see the context of the action. That's what we are looking for in mindfulness: we see the context. And once you see the context, all sorts of things fall into place automatically. Your awareness of the details you wish to communicate deepens. Your point of view broadens, which allows you to perceive how other people may look or respond to your message (we'll talk more about this aspect in a later section on audience analysis). Your tone changes. Through no additional conscious effort, you will go from sounding as if you are a panicked or irritated person who didn't give all the details to someone who is calm and collected even under the pressure of the situation. In other words that image we keep talking about improves, just by taking that Zen minute to focus.

Why the Zen method? Think about the world we live in. Instead of making our lives simpler, technology and social media often make our lives more difficult. People around us become increasingly self-absorbed, and self-focused; it's almost as if the focus and a picture narrows down to one point.

Think about Google Earth: we can see the big picture of the town and then through the manipulation of a scale bar, we can narrow down so that we suddenly see nothing but our own house and our own environment. That same sort of a narrowing of perspective and thought is pervasive in the modern working world. It creates anxiety. No matter what, modern business life can leave us feeling as if we're trying to juggle many plates in the air, certain we are dropping some, working frantically to make sure we catch at least a few. Even if we catch them all today, we're left with the feeling that we should have done better, could have caught more, and that there is something somewhere we didn't catch.

That nagging feeling increases the anxiety and we become more constricted, more focused on ourselves and our inabilities, and more looking into the future instead of dealing with what's in front of us today. My first mentor used to say that we needed to keep our heads where our feet are. She said that if we have one foot in yesterday, either by recalling what we were supposed to do yesterday and did not get done, or by regretting or reliving incidents and words and lack of perfect performance in the past, we diminished our abilities to perform well in the present.

By putting the other foot in the future, anxiety ridden and worried about what was going to come our way, the what ifs, the what abouts, and all the other doubts that plague us, we diminished our abilities to perform in the present even further. We diminish ourselves, we constrict ourselves, and we fail to see the bigger picture.

You'll know when you're in that spot. Your body will feel it. You will feel it tightening somewhere around your chest, with a buzz somewhere in your head, a lack of focus in your eyes, and a feeling that you need something. That feeling will keep pushing you to do more, be more, try more. But the body knows we can't.

That's why so many workers are addicted to doubleshot espressos and high-cost coffee: they feel their bodies need that boost. Yet Zen and its approach to life as well as its approach to business communication will tell you that the need for coffee, or sugar, or anything else is truly an illusion. Much like the people in Plato's cave, we see only the reflection of reality, not the reality of the present moment.

Emphasis on being in the present allows us to see perspective. It also allows us to see depth.

When we look at that Google Earth image of our house, we can still manipulate the screen to see bits and pieces of the house around us. But what we see is the snapshot that the Google Earth car took of our house when it went by. My college-student daughter and her friends were comparing notes and describing their houses when one of them got the bright idea to pull up pictures of their houses on Google Earth so they could know what they were talking about. Much to my daughter's surprise, the picture of our house showed an interesting feature: a back view of her dad painting the lawn furniture.

Now since he had painted the lawn furniture approximately eight months before she pulled up that picture, the view that Google Earth showed her was faulty. It was a memory, an illusion. Since then, the furniture has moved, the bushes have been trimmed, we've put in some flowers, and her dad has long since gone on to another project. But when we focus just on ourselves and one little incident, tinging it with one foot in yesterday and the other foot in tomorrow's anxiety, we don't see layers of depth.

Ever watch a computer move from a standard two-dimensional picture to a three-dimensional one? What appears to be a clear line suddenly expands, showing gaps and connections and an entirely different model of how the items on the two-dimensional picture are related. Being able to see that depth makes communicators great. It's what makes Peyton Manning and Tom Brady great quarterbacks; they don't just see the end zone and the guys running to catch the ball once they throw it; they see possibilities of movement. They see not just what is in front of them but what will be in front of them in a matter of seconds. How? They see the depth and connections of the now.

> Perspective is far more than the big picture. It encompasses the many layers and nuances and fluidity and change that occur with every action and every moment.

Without being aware of this perspective and depth, we usually will not communicate to our best, continuing that plate juggling act, still wondering if we can continue to pull off the act day by day.

Enter Zen. Zen is all about the moment. While Zen acknowledges yesterday, it is aware of that tomorrow may never come. And if it does come, it will bring things that most likely we cannot anticipate. We can anticipate only based on the information we have now, which may or may not be an illusion come tomorrow.

By focusing on the now, we lose anxiety. And we find ourselves truly focused on catching each spinning plate, and doing it well. The Dalai Lama has written extensively about the pleasures that one finds in every day at work and tasks by focusing on the moment. One example he uses is pleasure he finds in washing dishes. By focusing on the moment, he can truly feel the warmth of the water on his hands, the rainbows reflected in the bubbles of the soap, and the gratitude that he has had food to eat to put on the dishes. That's Zen focus.

CHAPTER 3

Honor Purpose and Identity

To every thing there is a season, and a time to every purpose under the heaven.

—Ecclesiastes 3:1

Ecclesiastes reminds us that everything has a purpose, whether we realize it or not. Communication, especially business communication, intends to convey information that will help an organization and individuals perform their duties and hopefully prosper. Although most of us have encountered someone we swear communicates only to hear himself speak, that person too has a purpose for talking.

The problem here is that the purpose for many of us is buried. It's covered up with all sorts of things we need to do and other thoughts. We often go through the motions, unaware of why we are really communicating. Remember the first day of the third grade, when your teacher had you write the infamous essay on how you spent your summer vacation? Many of us, clueless in our self-centeredness, thought the teacher wanted to know how each of us spent our summer days. In reality, the teacher's purpose was to get us back in the groove of school, thinking in an organized and logical manner, and working with a subject we had plenty of knowledge of, so we could be prepared for another school year.

So often we just tootle along, sending emails or leaving voice messages, thinking our purpose was in the act of sending that email or leaving that voice message. Yet the purpose is usually much deeper. Those who take the time to look at the proverbial bigger picture see the details—and they see that the purpose is much more than just to complete an action.

Burke's Pentad, a method of evaluating drama created by Kenneth Burke in 1945[1], offers the theory that things happen because of five elements: agent, act, scene, agency (or by what means), and purpose. How those elements are applied in a human action can vary; in the *Halloween* movies, for instance, the creepy scene and setting of October 31 supposedly move the agent to act as he does. When the rational part of the viewers is saying, "Why did she even open that door in the first place?" the intended message is that the scene was so powerful that the agent had no choice but to act as she did.

In other examples, however, the act chooses the agent. When the Germanwings airliner crashed in the French Alps in 2015, supposedly as the result of a suicide by the co-pilot, the only acceptable public spokesperson was Lufthansa CEO Carsten Spohr. Here, the agency—the means by which the co-pilot achieved his act—overshadowed the act itself, which then became so large that the only agent to handle the public communication had to be the CEO himself.

Often interpretations of the Pentad find that the purpose often lies in the agent. Yet purpose is rarely singular and surface. An organization, for instance, may have a *strategy*—a series of actions to be completed in various scenes by various agents. But that strategy came only after *strategic thinking*, which in itself could be possible only after deep critical thinking. Critical thinking, which is defined as *thinking about the validity of our thinking,* involves examination of our biases, our misperceptions, our distortions, and our blindness.

> Our real purpose for communicating may be hidden by those biases, misperceptions, distortions, and blindness as well. It may also be hidden by our view of ourselves and our reflection of how that purpose will make us look.

So we may send off a group email reminding people of a meeting the next day. Without due thought of our purpose, we may just look at it as "Yep, I told them when and where so I'm good" and hit Send. In this case, we as agent may give up our power as we act, in essence putting the email as one small bit of process that the scene—our busy day—demands, meeting the purpose of ticking off tasks on our to-do list.

---

[1] *See* Burke (1945).

But is the purpose just to remind them of the meeting? Why are we having the meeting anyway? Though many of us may feel our organizations meet just to meet, that's not really the purpose. Is the meeting's aim to decide on the next year's budget? To solve a problem? In either of these situations, each of the various agents who attend this meeting will have his or her own view of the scene, or his or her own agenda and belief of how the outcome should look. In crafting a reminder email, is the purpose also to remind others to bring supporting documentation with them? Or does your purpose include an unspoken reminder for all to leave their emotions at the door when the meeting commences?

To use an analogy, in Zen, a rose is still a rose, but it is also much more. Careful examination, or critical thought, of the rose allows you to see each petal, how it builds on its neighbors, is supported by a rather complicated combination of green parts (known as the sepal, the hypanthium, and the receptacle) that allows the beauty of the rose to happen. Close examination allows you to see all parts, even the small gold parts in its center (the anther and filament) that will help create this rose's progeny. A more panoramic but still detailed view of all these parts will show you the rose as a whole, with its gradations and flaws and what needs to be fixed for a more perfect rose.

Seeing all the parts of that meeting reminder, from the view of each player who will attend the meeting, will allow you to see who also may need to be there and hasn't been asked. It will allow you to create your communication in words most likely to bring the results you want. And it may show you that the email—the agency—isn't the best way to achieve an agreement on the budget. Maybe you need to make a call to each attendee, or visit invitees in person to remind them of the meeting. Understanding the purpose in its entirety will determine the act as well as the agency, not the other way around.

And maybe you aren't the best person to send the email. Would the scene and acts be more down to business if the email came from someone with more authority than you? Less authority? Only careful analysis of the purpose can tell you that.

In October 2013, when budget disagreements ground the U.S. government to a halt, five Congresswomen saw beyond their parties' stated purpose of winning over their opponents and having their own acts approved. Stating later that while they were aware that members of both political parties saw their movements as threats to the states they served, these women saw that the real purpose of how they needed to act was to help the people the shutdown was hurting. The purpose of the government, they said, was not to be mired down in wrangling over who was right, but to provide for the people.

It takes a strong understanding of others around you to be able to realize that maybe what you've been told is the purpose really isn't. And it takes a strong sense of personal identity to know when to act against a simplistic and deceptively stated purpose. It also takes a deep understanding of yourself to know whether, despite what appears to indicate you need to act, you really aren't the right one to do something. Knowledge of yourself and your role in the greater scheme of the corporation isn't employed best only in Burke's Pentad; knowing who you are and the role you play in any communication can help ensure your communication makes the point you intend.

Who Are You Anyway?

Who are you? Ask most Americans that question and you will get an answer that goes somewhat like this one: "My name is Jane Smith and I am a manager at XYZ corporation." If pushed a little further, we may add our parental or marital status; we may also add something we like to do.

But in answering this way, we are not only identifying mostly by what we do but identifying in a vacuum that is all about us. We're not answering in how our lives are part of the whole that surrounds us. Unfortunately, most of us communicate in that identity. We may identify at one particular moment something such as "I am Jane Smith the manager of Joe White who has just lost us a great client." What we may not recognize in this identification is that our emotions color how we see ourselves. Or that those emotions narrow our perspective to one small and often incorrect conclusion.

Zen teaches us that we are a part of all that we have met, and that our own identity is not just our own actions and being but part of all that surrounds us.

So Jane isn't just a manager at XYZ corporation, who happens to be married, has two kids, and likes to play tennis. Jane as manager is the role model for those who report to her as well as for her children. She is the partner to her peers as they help the corporation achieve its mission. She is the mentor to those who report to her as well as perhaps to others in the organization. She is the one who has expert knowledge in a particular area that affects all employees. She is the face of the organization for clients and vendors she deals with directly; she is the face of her department to executives in her company. She is the decision-maker, the purchaser, the rewarder, the motivator, the demotivator, and often the barometer or one who sets the emotional and ethical culture for her department.

In other words, Jane is a lot more than her initial identification of herself. And when she takes a step back to see the larger view of that actual identity, how she communicates will change.

Every action has an opposite reaction, and those reactions can have consequences. If, for instance, Jane sees herself only as "I am Jane Smith the manager of Joe White who has just lost us a great client," she may think about Joe in an angry manner and then communicate with him in a manner that reflects poorly not only on who she is but poorly on who she thinks he is. Joe may be a good employee who has made one bad move, but that doesn't mean he is all bad. And that doesn't mean that he needs to be treated poorly. The result of that treatment won't be good for anyone, not even the client.

Traditional negotiation training teaches that the negotiator who leaves emotional reaction out of the negotiation achieves far more and far better value for all parties.

The technique for leaving out that emotion is pure Zen method: the negotiator acknowledges the emotion that is stirred in him by the circumstances and communications, but he does not act on it. He acknowledges it and analyzes not only why he feels the way he does but what consequences that emotion could have on his larger goal. And he then views that emotional reaction in a larger scope, seeing it as only a part of the whole scheme of the negotiation rather than the trigger for the negotiation's next move.

This technique, often summed up as *name it, claim it, and reframe it*, allows him to see a bigger picture and a brighter goal. He becomes enlightened as to the long-term possibilities while his sense of self retreats to be equal to that of how he views the others in his negotiation.

If one presses Jane about who she wants to be, she may answer that she wants to be a good manager. She may say she wants to be the CFO as well; that depends on Jane herself. But implied in those terms, be they the adjective *good* or the position *CFO*, really what she means she wants to be is successful. Jane's definition of being successful may mean highly paid, but unless she is really shallow the pay is only a portion of what she means. She most likely means she wants to understand as well as be understood, motivated, motivating, and happy. She wants to shine and be a leader and have purpose in her life and actions.

And by recognizing her larger identity and connectedness to all things, including that client that Joe presumably lost, she gains compassion.

True wisdom is having compassion for all things, including one's self—or as radio show *Prairie Home Companion* host Garrison Keeler puts it, being kind to those who may deserve it the least. Compassion allows understanding.

> Identifying in a larger sense before one communicates ensures compassionate communication and concrete communication. And that is a huge step toward communicating with wisdom.

And admit it: you don't delete unopened emails from people you consider wise, do you?

The Dancing Icons, or What Image Do You Want to Send?

A chief nursing officer of a large hospital in a large city tells the story of a nurse manager whose unawareness of her identity in the organization led to chaos and decreased patient care. This particular nurse manager was well educated and, although fairly young, had extensive professional experience in her field. Her department attracted highly trained specialized nurses, so when the CNO began noticing the significant turnover in this department, she at first attributed it to the nurses moving for pay increases. But when she also started noticing that the patient care scores were lower than expected in this department, she started wondering what was up and began conducting the exit interviews for this department herself, in person.

The first few interviews yielded nothing but the fact that the nurses who were leaving were guarded about their reasons for doing so. The third interviewee, however, was more than willing to discuss why she was leaving: she was tired of being talked to "like a piece of dirt" by a "spoiled child." Moreover, she pulled out her smartphone and showed the CNO an email from the nurse manager to illustrate her point. The email read as follows:

> *I watched you work yesterday. You were too slow in getting the vitals and you were rude to the patient's family. Fix this immediately or I will write you up.*

The email was concluded by a series of smiley faces that were animated to dance. (I kid you not.)

When confronted by the CNO about this email, the nurse manager was surprised that the nurse had taken offense to it. "I was just giving her daily feedback," she said; "that's good managerial practice, according to training I've had. And she shouldn't have taken it so seriously. I mean, that's why I added the smiley faces: so she would know that this was a basic 'here's what you are doing' email and that in general she was doing a good job."

Indeed.

The issue here is that of the old saw about knowing all of the words but knowing nothing of the meaning. The nurse manager was right in that giving daily feedback is a best practice—but how one gives that feedback, as well as the intent of that feedback, is much more crucial in the long run for a department's success than the actual point being discussed. The nurse manager didn't look at the bigger scope of the goal or the scene in which she was communicating. She also surely didn't think about what kind of image those dancing smiley faces would send to her employees. Even if she had written the perfect email to achieve her goals, her audience would see those dancing smiley faces as sarcastic or as coming from someone not to be taken seriously.

As Robert Tannenbaum[2] pointed out in 1958 in *The Harvard Business Review*, all leadership communication falls into one of four types: *tell, sell, join, and consult.* Tannebaum, and Mary Munter (1992)[3] after him, explain that you tell when you are in complete command of the information. You sell when you want to persuade others that your ideas are valid. You join when you connect your ideas to those of another person to build something larger than the ideas that each of you has on your own. And you consult when you offer insight or experience on a subject or an action.

Usually, the *tell* approach is the least effective, yet it is the one used most often by poor or inexperienced managers. These novices usually operate in the I mode: they think, *I know the information, and I know what*

---

[2]See Robert and Schmidt (1958).
[3]See Muntur (1992).

I want to say, so I am in control of the information, so I can tell my audience what I want them to know. Do you hear the fallacy in thought here?

We know from our Zen approach that operating in I mode will shoot you in the foot every single time.

In I mode, you've narrowed the scope of how you view the situation, setting yourself up to be blind to other possibilities and information that may pertain to the situation: Very rarely do we know everything in a situation enough to say we are in complete command of the information. Moreover, you're not in complete control of the information even though you may know all aspects of the situation. In 99 percent of all communication, you are not the only one involved. Therefore, someone else exists in this exchange—and you don't have control over how that person will process or react to the information.

You can walk into a crowded movie theater and yell Fire! and be pretty certain of how people will process and react to that communication.But without careful thought and audience analysis, using *tell* rarely works. Even grasping that reality, we fall into traps where we think we have control. We consider the audience, and then we write small scripts in our heads that convince us that our audience will react a certain way once we tell. The problem is that we don't share those scripts. Therefore, other people rarely know their lines—they may not know how you see their roles, much less when you have determined they should appear on stage. So we start telling, thinking that we are gracious and generous and offering the products of our minds. And we wind up becoming Oz the Great and Terrible—the talking green head who pontificates like the speaker in T.S. Eliot's Wasteland: *I will tell you all; I shall tell you all*—whether or not anyone wants to hear it.

Unfortunately, *tell* is the form that usually makes people resentful and often carries with it an unpleasant tone. It's one-way speech, because the speaker wants no feedback or any input from the other person; the speaker just wants action from the listener, and it'd better be exactly the action we tell the listener to take.

In using *tell*, we become autocratic and querulous, and demanding without meaning to. And the result echoes another quote from the

Wasteland: *I will show you fear in a handful of dust.* Remember that old joke about the Marines? When the sergeant says jump, your next move is to ask how high? And you don't stop jumping until you are told to? Keep that image in mind; that's *tell*.

Most of us, however, are not Marines, and except on the battle field, even the Corps was never that rigid. One of the major factors that built the Corps to be the few, the proud, and the brave is their respect for each other; the Corps is demanding and it holds its members to the highest standards of the U.S. military, but it does so by building some of the strongest bonds and loyalty in organizations today. Once a Marine, always a Marine; one never stops being a Marine, even after discharge—those bonds and loyalty remain.

Compare that with the fact that people job hop not nearly as much to earn more money as they do to get away from an unpleasant work environment; it's said that people don't leave a job—they leave a supervisor who treated them poorly. My guess is that part of that poor treatment is a constant use of *tell* that demoralizes even the most eager employee.

And those of us who feel entitled to use *tell* in most situations would do well to remember Newton's Third Law: When one body exerts a force on a second body, the second body simultaneously exerts a force equal in magnitude and opposite in direction on the first body. Note that last part: those who hear *tell* when *tell* isn't appropriate push back. Want something to change? Don't tell someone to change. Whatever you want will fail due to the method of delivery. It will backfire on you.

Yet *tell* is effective in certain situations. For safety measures, as in the fire example, *tell* is the only way to fly. And in true emergencies, or in training for those emergencies, we want telling. But that's pretty much it. Want better results? Try a different approach.

Getting people to accept the products of our minds is what most of us do all day long, even if we don't work in sales. That's why the second method works much better. It's called *selling*. With this technique, you convince the other party that your message is appropriate. The late great William Buckley reportedly once said that all communication is persuasive in nature. Even in such a simple statement as, "it's a pretty day outside" you sell the idea that the day is indeed pretty. Some may argue that asking another person how her day was is just conversation; but by asking, you are selling the idea that you care about the person and her answer.

However, when you sell, remember to sell benefits, not features. Just because the latest smartphone has a personal assistant and sixty innate apps doesn't mean it will serve me; you can list the features and I will walk right on by. That's telling, not selling. But if you persuade me of how that personal assistant can benefit me, and how those apps can make my life a bit easier, then those are benefits—and you have sold. You have persuaded me.

In other words, remember that the best thing you can do to send any kind of message is remember the "what's in it for me?" approach for communicating with the audience. (We'll delve more deeply into this approach in a later chapter.)

The third type of communication is called *joining*. You use this technique when you need people to work with you according to your point of view. This technique is especially powerful in the workplace because people want to think that they're in control and they're not being micromanaged. In a Zen approach, *join* means you see yourself as one of them. You see yourself as part of all this around you. The perspective widens, grows deeper, adds layers of understanding. This approach is powerful because it will allow you and the audience to see all the details that perhaps you would not see from the sell or tell point of view.

The final and extremely powerful approach is called *consulting*. Often those who are in a position of power think that because they own the decision, they don't need to consult. They say things such as "I hold all the information and I make the decisions, so I tell you what to do."

Oh, really?

How do you know you have *all* the information? You may have what you have been able to gather, or at least all that the others want you to have. Rarely do employees tell the CEO every small detail—although those details may have huge implications on the decision. The U.S. has lost not one but two space shuttles that way: for a variety of reasons, information about possible malfunctions in the equipment didn't make it to the decision-makers. As a result, the decision-makers *told*—with disastrous results.

Moreover, telling rarely gets results, as we have pointed out.

Zen will encourage you to think about the possible results of telling: Like the rock that remains in the river, no matter how hard the water bears down on it, the rock remains steadfast. It may erode, it may diminish, and eventually it may be swept away, but never does it become liquid and flow exactly as the river does.

People act like that rock. Enduring constant telling may erode their work ethics and diminish their enthusiasm, and they may eventually have had enough and leave. But the rush of the telling always has to go around them. And if you are the one doing the telling, sooner or later, you will find yourself exhausted. Why? Except in rare cases, this approach simply doesn't work.

In consulting, you present your information and case. You build a presentation of what is known as a *win-win*; this approach asks you to sell benefits, not features, for the change not only you but for the listener. Then you ask the other person for his information and input. You have to listen carefully as he speaks; perhaps you have to get past some venting or some emotional outbursts. But what always happens is that you gain information you did not have before, which in turn allows you to build a better decision. Consulting incorporates the best of the three previous methods, so your result is three times as strong. Why? You are actually allowing the other person to communicate your message to himself. By doing so, you allow him the power to consider many of the points of your message—which has deep and powerful internal impact on his psyche.

You offer respect and honor—two cardinal principals of Zen—and what you usually get is respect and honor in return.

Much better than dancing smiley faces, don't you think?

CHAPTER 4

Honor Your Goals

"Would you tell me, please, which way I ought to go from here?"
"That depends a good deal on where you want to get to."
"I don't much care where —"
"Then it doesn't matter which way you go."
— Lewis Carroll, *Alice in Wonderland*

Having goals in business communications seems one of those "well, duh" kind of ideas. Yet having goals also seems contrary to the Zen idea of living in the moment. The truth is that goals and Zen do coincide; once you have decided your focus and purpose, you need to decide what to do with them. Although just sitting and letting things be, watching the world go by, sounds enticing, it is not one of the steps to Enlightenment.

A great deal of process and thinking is involved in reaching *Satori*, which is the Zen term for perfect enlightenment about the world around us.

On the other hand, most of us who work in the 21st century American workforce have been inundated with what is known as SMART goals: in other words, goals that are strategic, measureable, achievable, relevant, and time-bound. While the intent in the acronym is to help us take our skills to a higher level, we humans usually botch the process. Why? Well, for one, we've been goaled to death. Often our performance evaluations and pay are tied to how many times we speak with a client or how many committees we serve on. But using numbers to determine whether we have achieved a rating of "exceeds expectations" or even a mere "meets expectations" is just counting. It's quantitative, not qualitative. It doesn't tell how well we did something, only that we did it often.

So we could speak to 10,000 clients and look really good and appear to have blown our target goal out of the water. But if we speak to them all in a really weak manner with poor communication skills, we haven't done anything productive. We haven't helped the company. We've just done the thing a lot.

Which leads us to another reason humans rarely reach *Satori*: we scam the goal system. Faced with having to do something many times in order to be considered competent, we don't think about perfecting even one repetition of the act. Instead, we choose what is easy for us to do, so doing it a lot won't take much effort.

Or we embrace the moment as a flight of what could be and set impossible goals such as *lose 30 pounds, take up racewalking, learn to play the tuba, and climb Mount Kilimanjaro within six months.* These goals usually arise from a wish to be someone quite different from who we are. They don't take into account what changes in us will have to occur in order for us to take the first step toward these goals (*what do you mean, I have to give up my three-times-daily caramel latte? And forget walking today; it's raining.*) Such goals usually fail, mainly because we have not considered the scene, the agency, the purpose, or even ourselves in making them. We may not be aware we are scamming the goal system, but we are.

So we react in our human ways. As one shrewd observer pointed out, we are humans being and not humans doing, no matter how we behave. And as Art Markham, University of Texas professor of psychology and marketing, points out in his book *Smart Change,* our brains are lazy. They are programmed to minimize the amount of time and energy we have to expend on anything (p. 35).[1] So what we do is avoid having to change behavior by adding so many abstractions and good intentions that the actual issue becomes clouded—and we can rest easy, knowing that doing anything about that issue is going to be hard. And if it is hard, then we can talk about how hard our goals are—more of the "I" stuff, as in *look at me, look at what goals I have set for myself*—and avoid the issue altogether.

Unfortunately, this view of goals and goal-setting becomes just more clutter, more stuff that lets us hide from true communication and *Satori*. Quantity is never quality, and never more so in communication. Remember

---

[1]See Markham (2014).

that concept of getting the I out of your communication? If you're so fo-cused on the idea that "I have to make six calls today" that the amount becomes more important than the substance, you have not only lost your Zen but also lost the basic idea of why you communicate in the first place.

Take, for example, the story of Jenny, an up-and-coming mid-level manager who was entrusted with managing a group project that was one as-pect of a plan that affected the overall company. Jenny welcomed the oppor-tunity with the proverbial open arms. In her initial meetings with her boss, he explained that he wanted her to keep him in the loop as far as what was going on, but that he wouldn't micromanage; it would be up to her to tell him when he was needed to approve what the group had done. Only then would he give permission for Jenny to decide what the team was to do next.

The project team caught Jenny's enthusiasm and finished their work ahead of schedule. They especially liked the no-micromanaging part of their task. Proud of them, Jenny spent two hours writing up their work in an Excel and graph format, attaching it to a short email that said, "*Hi, Mike, Here's an analysis of what we have done so far. We welcome your comments.*" Two hours later, the boss sent a two-word reply: *Good work.* Nothing was said about whether he had approved what they had done in its entirety, whether he wanted more detail or development, or even whether he had given permission for them to move on.

Jenny and the team sat puzzled for a few days. Then Jenny added more details to the report and sent it again, attached to another email that said *Hi, Mike, I've added some more details to the report. Let me know what you think.*" A few hours later, the boss replied: *Keep up the good work!*

Jenny emailed the boss's assistant to set up a face-to-face meeting, where she asked him if he had read her reports. Yes, he acknowledged, he did. Did he approve of what they had done? Again the answer was yes. Finally, after some more dancing around on Jenny's part, the boss gently asked her, "What exactly is your goal for this meeting?" When Jenny answered, "to get your permission for us to move on," the boss said, "You could have asked me that in an email." Jenny then said that she had thought she had done so with the two emails and attached reports, to which the boss replied, "If your goal was to have me give permission, you should have asked me for that in those exact words in the emails. I thought you were just keeping me in the loop."

Shamefaced at having wasted the team's and her boss's time, Jenny returned to her team to tell them that they had received permission to move on. But stalled by the long delay, the team never regained its initial enthusiasm and finished the next step of the project behind schedule, kissing its effectiveness—and Jenny's possible promotion—good-bye.

This story has two morals:

1. **Data isn't communication.** You can distribute all the graphs and spreadsheets you want, but unless you tell the recipients what you want them to do with the information, most likely they will take a quick look at the numbers and data, nod their heads, retain a small fraction of the information, and forget most of it, moving on with their own lives and projects. You have to tell the readers why you are showing them data or giving them information; just because it makes sense to you, and helps you check off an item on your yearly SMART goal list, doesn't mean that the information is of value to anyone else. That is, unless you have told them how it can be and what you want them to do with it.

2. **The email isn't the afterthought to the attachment.** The attachment is the afterthought to the email. This is especially true when the attachment contains a lot of data. Ever get one of those emails that have no words in them at all, just an attachment? How irritated do you become when you get one of those? The empty message means having to stop your train of thought, open the attachment, scan the attachment, try to make sense of what it is supposed to tell you, and then spend more time trying to figure out what the sender wanted you to do with the information.

Senders of empty emails and the ones with the cryptic one or two sentences that merely announce the attachment exhibit the opposite of the Zen concept of removing the self. The senders may be unaware that their emails are self-centered, but they are: in their hurry to get out the email and demonstrate the sender's productivity, they wind up stealing time and energy from the readers, which is usually the last thing they should wish to do.

What Jenny could have achieved is better communication by using a Zen approach in both the emails and the face-to-face meeting. To do so, first take a deep breath, a move that sounds cheesy but in actuality allows your focus to widen. Now look at your overall surroundings, noting the other players in the environment.

Too often we get so caught up in our own stuff, intent in charging at our own need to knock down the obstacles and clutter we see in front of us, that we fail to see that a widened focus reveals a much easier and simpler way to progress along our paths.

Now ask yourself, *What do I want to happen as a result of this communication?* Sometimes that's a hard question, sometimes it isn't. Sometimes the answer is a simple sentence; had Jenny asked herself, *What do I want to happen as a result of my sending Mike this report?* She could have answered *I want him to grant permission to move on to the next stage.* If the answer is one simple sentence, then you move on to the next step in basic Zen goal setting: setting the intention. Now ask yourself *Have I asked clearly and simply for what I want?* Here's where most of us go wrong. We think we have asked, but imply our request, just as Jenny did. We expect that the receiver knows what we are talking about. We don't ask.

And here's where the whole SMART goal thing is misconstrued and can go wrong. We focus so finely on ourselves that we don't see how we are getting in our own way. We put so much importance on the action that we don't think about how the action can be perceived and whether it truly will advance us to our goal. SMART goals have their place. But considered in a Zen manner, they aren't enough. Coupling them with two Zen questions can help improve not only these goals but what they can attain for you and the organization you work for:

"Have I clarified the final intent of this goal to myself as well as to others?"

"Have I considered the environment in which I intend this goal to take place?"

Asking yourself these two questions can lead you to far better results every time.

Let's explore these ideas a bit further. Asking yourself "Have I clarified the final intent of this goal to myself as well as to others?" has four main parts to it. The best place to start in addressing the parts is in the middle. In Zen, one always starts with what is in front of you, and then moves out to consider what is on the periphery. Look at the word *final intent*. You have to use that word *final*. You might think that your goal—your intent—is to send off the report. But it isn't. If hitting the send button was a goal, we would all be extra-high performers. Sending off the report is an action toward the goal, but it doesn't address the final intent of the goal. What we have to do is think about the whole process of each action until there isn't an action left.

How? Imagine each step after you hit Send. What will then happen? The email will arrive in someone's inbox—or not, because there's always a chance of things being lost in cyberspace. But let's say that it does. Then what?

A July 2012 McKinsey Global Institute report found that the average knowledge worker spent 14 hours a week, or 28 percent of his work week, on email.[2] Think about that. We are inundated with email. People send us everything from notices that cake is in the breakroom to interoffice newsletters that mainly tell us who's having a birthday. This average worker, however, has to be on top of these frequent messages. He has to scan through them all, prioritize which ones he wants to read when, and then again quickly scan the message to see what is required of him. (And then realize that the cake email came from a different company location and the cake is only in the office in Pittsburgh.)

Now imagine the result you want; if you are Jenny, you want the boss to approve the project. But is that all you want? And is it in the form that you want it? Imagine how this approval could happen: he could say to himself, *OK, time to move on*, and then go to the next email, meaning to reply later—and possibly forgetting to do so or doing so much later than you desired. Do you need only verbal approval, or would written approval make taking the next steps easier down the road?

So let's say that what you really want is to have the boss immediately respond with *You have permission to move to the next stage of the project.* If that's your final intent, that's what you focus on. You have set the final

---

[2] See McKinsey Global Institute (2012).

intention of the goal. And you have clarified to yourself that is what you want. Often we also think that because we have clarified the goal to ourselves, naturally we have clarified the goals to others. Because that isn't often the case, we need to move on to the second question: "Have I considered the environment in which I intend this goal to take place?"

Computers are marvelous inventions. But they are also the ultimate narcissistic tool; we stare at their screens so much that we lose awareness of those around us. They trick us into believing that we are all that is important and that our words are clear because we said so. Think about it; the computer screen always loves us. It never frowns at us, never interrupts, never questions. It will occasionally shut down, but when it starts back up, it doesn't yell at us. It offers much to distract us, so that when we go back to what we need to be doing, we may not take into account a lapse in continuity of thought. In fact, as Adam Gopnik implies in his clever novel *The King in the Window*, if we're not careful, these little devils can steal our souls. [3]

So as we set out goals, we need to revisit that good old Zen practice of removing ourselves from the picture for a moment. Let's get that self-centered solipsism out of the way for second. We've envisioned what we want to happen when we hit Send—but have we envisioned what may happen when the other person gets that familiar ping announcing a new message?

This consideration of the larger environment may be as simple as taking three seconds to remember that the person you need information from ASAP may be out of town in training. If so, you're not likely to get that information any time soon. It may be a little more complicated, as in realizing that the person you're contacting may be under a deadline to finish a huge report, which means that either she won't be looking at her inbox at all or will be irritated that you had the gall to ask her to take a minute out of her already tight timeline to attend to your needs.

Or maybe something is going on in the department or company that may make your goal come across as inconsiderate or even crass. Asking for permission to take your team to the next step of a project may not be exactly wise when your boss is considering budget cuts, for instance. You may still need his permission, but being aware of his situation and

[3]See Gopnik (2005).

his operating environment may convince you to alter your goal a bit. You might, for instance, more effectively craft your message by acknowledging your boss's current situation and explaining why you are bothering him. This blithe wording likely will not achieve your purpose:

> *Hi, Mike, we think we've knocked stage one out of the park and would love for you to tell us to start stage two ASAP.*

Instead, you could craft your goal to fit within the needs of the organization:

> *Hi, Mike, I realize this isn't the best time to ask you anything, but the team and I are wondering if we should start planning stage 2. I've attached a report that breaks down all that we have done as well as our analysis of those actions. If you have time to read it in the next 48 hours and can give me the go-ahead or at least some direction, that would be wonderful. That way the team can keep their momentum if we are indeed going forward. Let me know if you need anything or any help that I can offer.*

With such a reworded message, you're not coming across as just me-centered. You'll also note that in this reworded email, you've actually communicated two goals: (1) you need his permission, and (2) in this environment, you and the team want to know if the project—and your team—is still part of the company's plan.

This leads to another important aspect of goal setting: you can have several layers of goals in one message. Your main goal, known as the *primary* goal, is always present. But you can also have a *secondary* goal, as the situation above illustrates. You could also have a *tertiary* goal, which is usually a minor goal that is embedded in the previous two. Here again taking those few seconds to evaluate the environment you're communicating in will help you recognize what you should do. Maybe you're the boss, and you need to send Jenny and her crew the go-ahead for stage two, but you also need to send the message that while the company may be making huge cuts in operating expenses you are relying on their enthusiasm and professionalism to continue. In this manner, the go-ahead is the primary goal while the motivational message is the secondary goal. By acknowledging the offer of help—and perhaps delegating a task that would help you—you also meet a tertiary goal of reassuring Jenny that her job at least is not in jeopardy.

All This Sounds Like Strategy

It is. Part of a Zen approach is thinking about the best way to proceed on your path. Taking the path of least resistance is usually the smarter way to travel. Note that as you read the preceding sentence, read it in the Zen manner: *not about you.* We're not necessarily talking about you resisting less; perhaps what you need here is the receiver taking the path of least resistance. Setting up a situation of acknowledging the reader and his working environment lowers emotional walls, which in turn increases your chances of a favorable outcome. Be aware, however, that you can overthink the choice, which leads to indecision.

> Stay true to your purpose and your sense of identity, recognizing the scene and the agency, and the way will become clear.

As Yogi Berra said, when you come to a fork in the road, take it. The elements we've considered in this chapter, plus an understanding of your audience, will help you achieve your goals.

CHAPTER 5

Honor the Audience

No man is an island.

—John Donne

Ok. You may be saying. I get it; it's not about me. But who is it about?

Ah. That is the appropriate question, grasshopper.

Good communication is like good ballroom dancing: one person leads, intending for the other person to look great and graceful. Yes, the one who leads looks great as well. Yet most people in the know realize that he—or she, as so often happens—is the one responsible for the flair and the fun. The leader of the couple signals his intent and his plan so that the follower can go where she is supposed to go. In time. On beat. And never miss a step.

> That's what you want in good Zen communication: that your audience goes with you in time and space to where you want to go. Meeting the goal and accomplishing the psychic bond that happens when two people understand each other perfectly.

If you've ever been in a country honkytonk bar where the crowd is into line dancing, you will also recognize that if the whole crowd is dancing on step and not crashing into each other, a good leader is also usually at work. When you give people the tools and knowledge of the steps, model it for them, and signal clearly what you want them to do, you can move mountains.

So, as a good communicator, just like a good dancer, you have to be aware of and accept the followers' strengths and weaknesses. And you accommodate, no matter how much you may not want to. The success of the dance—like the success of the communication—depends on your doing so. Otherwise you are out there wind dancing, all alone in your own world, full of your own sounds and possible fury, and, as Shakespeare pointed out, signifying nothing.

Like all Zen concepts, explaining how to adapt to your audience is best accomplished by a story.

I live on a corner, where the driveway is on a side street away from the front door. The most convenient entrance, therefore, is through the back and into the kitchen. And every day, my family comes home through that kitchen door, kicks off their shoes, and dumps their backpacks and other belongings in the kitchen chairs and on the kitchen table.

This whole process drives me crazy. I need to move their books, their keys, their lunch boxes, gym bags, and a whole host of other things to cook dinner. I usually trip over their shoes. And almost every single day my message in my head is, "How many times do I have to tell you? Don't put this stuff there!" And sometimes I am in my own little box, aware of no one and nothing but myself, and I say that exact message in those exact words. And every single time that I do, it backfires on me. Because my message was crafted all about me, my family members each retreat in their own little worlds and entrench themselves there: if I communicate in a way that says it is all about me, well, by gum, they are going to make it all about them. Not only do I get pushback and possible attitude, but I still wind up having to pick up everything anyway.

This is not good Zen communication. And the worst part is that no matter how many times I send the message that way, their reaction never gets more favorable. It's a lesson I often have to relearn.

Yet when I am on my game and in my good Zen communication mode, I know that saying that message just the way I thought it is going to back-fire on me. Instead I need to think about my goals. What do I really want? I know what I mean by "get these things out of here!" But they don't. I know all of the tangential items and meanings and nuances and everything else that I intend in that message in my head. They do not. So I have to think about what is my real goal. I then go through the steps that we've just talked about. I also know I have three very different people who are hearing the message—I need to tailor my message in a different way for each one.

But Isn't This a Lot of Work?

Yes. So is dealing with attitudes and picking up after everyone. What Zen communication teaches us is that careful investment in delivering the message in a way each one in the audience understands is an investment in a positive goal. In negotiation theory, it's called finding communal goals and establishing bonds. By spending the few moments it takes to decide what my true goal is, understand who my audience is and what's in it for them, I am investing at the beginning. I'm not paying accrued emotional interest on top of doing the work after the poorly constructed message. I am investing in harmony—and in getting what I want.

Why? Because only by identifying my real goal, and then identifying and analyzing my audience, will I be successful. What do I really want here? I want the shoes in the closets in their room, or put under the dresser, out of the way. I want the keys hung up by the back door so we don't have to hunt for them in the morning. And I want the backpacks over in the corner where the kids can grab them later to do homework. I want the lunchboxes emptied and the containers put in the dishwasher. I want the table clear and a clean canvas for me to start the ever-present work of feeding my family.

Is any of that in the message "How many times do I have to tell you? Don't put this stuff there!"? I didn't think so. And if I try to explain what I mean by that message, all they are going to hear is that teacher noise from the Peanuts specials: *waa waa waa*. I blew the message and their willingness to hear me with that shoot-from-the-hip self-centered focus. What should I do?

Let's continue with my example. We know that shooting from the hip with my internal thought isn't going to work. I can also say, "Pick up your shoes." And three different things will happen, depending on which of my three family members I say it to. My husband, who means well will reach down, pick up his shoes, and put them on the nearest flat surface that is not the floor. That may be one of the kitchen chairs, which does not help me any at all. He's been known to put the shoes on the table, which then makes even more work for me. Or he may just move them to the corner of the room, which doesn't help me meet my goal either.

My college-aged daughter, who seems to always be busy, on overload, wanting to please, but always with her mind somewhere else, will say, "Sure, mom, I'll get to it in just a moment." And she means to. The problem is she becomes involved in a text from her friend, her homework, her intent to go out and run, or something else that is important in her teenage life, and she will forget. Picking up shoes really is on the periphery of her life and while it means something to me, with all of the mix that she has going on, it really does not mean anything to her.

What usually happens is that the shoes and backpack and keys will stay where they first landed. I may even say five more times "Please pick up the shoes" and nothing happens. I become frustrated, which upsets my Zen calm, and then either I do the work myself and fume about it, which wastes my energy far past what I would have used to do the actual work of picking up the items, or I revert to that I mode and deliver a scathing message that accomplishes nothing. (See the paragraph above on sending verbatim the message in your head. It still doesn't work.)

My teenaged son really wants to please. And when I say, "pick up your shoes," he'll come pick them up and put them down somewhere not far from where they were. He has a short attention span, just like his sister, mainly because he has a lot going on in his life as well. He does not want to be disobedient—but he's literal. He picked up the shoes, didn't he? He's just doing what I told him to do. He can't help it that I didn't craft my message so that the audience understood all that I meant by that remark.

Now if I analyze all three of my audiences then I realize I need to craft my message in a different manner. My husband, bless him, has been married to me for very long time. He has learned quickly that the simplest way for him to proceed with his own work and agenda is to do what I've asked him to do—and like my son, that's what he does, exactly what I said. However, that does not always guarantee that I get what I want.

Like many employees who have many things to do for many different people, my daughter sometimes does not see what I'm asking her to do as important in her grand picture as it does to me. And my son is like a junior employee brand-new to the organization: he's too new to the job to really see what my goals are. My husband, also known as my business partner, has his own strategies and therefore needs to know that this action meets our overall common goals. The problem isn't them. The problem is me. I haven't considered them as people with needs and duties other than jumping to my own commands. And without that analysis, my communication and its intent fail.

Analyzing your audience really does come down to one main thing: being aware of the other person's existence.

Remember when we get out of that I box, we have to know this other person exists. We no longer function as a middle-schooler, full of angst and inward focus. We function as calm, capable, and reasonable beings, willing to work for the common good of our organization and ourselves.

But How Do You Analyze?

To do so, you ask yourself some questions. It's not enough just to know that the person that you're writing to or talking to is Mary Smith. You have to consider *her*. That means you have to know several things about her, such as what's going on with Mary. What is happening in her life right now? Who all else is asking her to do things? What's her main function? What's her background? Is she going to have time to pay attention to you and your message right now, or should you wait a few hours—or a day? How does she interact with people? Does she listen with one hand on her smartphone, checking her email, or does she write down notes as you talk?

All of this understanding allows your picture of Mary to develop sharply. You consider her. You don't judge her. You just focus on her—almost as if you have a movie that is taking a wide panoramic shot of her. That way you can see how your message will play in the larger picture of what's going on in her life.

The second question you ask yourself is "What's Mary's relationship to me? Who is she? Is she is my peer? My subordinate who may be a little nervous about receiving a message from me? Is she positioned in authority above me?" You need to think about how you're going to work your message for each of these different positions. This second question allows you to ask how Mary will relate to you—and how will she feel about this relationship. The answers to this one will help you decide the tone of your message.

The third question you ask yourself when analyzing your audience is "What is Mary's relationship to the material I'm about to present? Is the material something she already knows very well? Or is it something that's brand-new to her?" Perhaps if you are an IT specialist or research chemist, if you are sending the material to someone else who is also in your own field, you will have an easier time explaining the material than you would if you had to send the same material to someone in PR or marketing. The person in your field will be close and familiar with the material—but someone else won't.

You also need to know what Mary's relationship is to the message. This is especially important when you consider the emotional response she probably will have to it. Think about whether a message is going to stir a negative emotional response in her. If it is, that will determine which media to send your message—something we will discuss in a later chapter. Ask yourself as well how she will use this material that you are providing. If she needs it to make a decision, have you given all of the points she needs? Imagine Mary's face as she reads the message, and picture yourself watching her as tries to respond to the message. Doing so will help you craft that message to serve the best purpose it can.

The last question you ask yourself when you're analyzing your audience is "What are this person's strengths and weaknesses?" I don't necessarily mean is Mary a good writer or good with numbers, although that also helps you get a full picture of who she is. What I mean by this is someone who is very socially intelligent will be very aware of how information is processed through different people. She will see many nuances and aspects to your message, more so than someone who is strongly analytical and who relies on facts alone; she will innately understand what you intend to say even if you didn't say it well. Does she have a very strong emotional intelligence? If so, you may have to be more careful of the emotional impact and nuances in the words you choose. She may be easily offended or take statements in a way that you did not intend. If she is high in standard logical and rational intelligence, she'll want to see how one step leads to another. A printable to-do or how-we-got-here list will work better than anything else to help her process information.

Now, while it seems as if following every one of these techniques will take a long time, in reality the process doesn't take more than about one or two minutes. The first time you actually think through writing to Mary will take the longest. After that, all you need to do is recall your thoughts; perhaps keeping notes in your contacts file will help. Understanding and honoring the audience is such a crucial part of communicating that having these understandings—and notes about what worked and what you didn't understand—will help assure that each subsequent communication is quicker and more successful. Plus, it builds your awareness of those and the world around you.

We have to stop here and talk about listening. Not hearing—*listening*. We are so inundated daily with sounds no matter where we go. We may be outside and hear the birds—but we're just as likely to hear jackhammers in traffic. When we're in the grocery store, for instance, we hear piped-in music, advertisements, and other people talking. We even hear other people's loud conversations on their cell phones.

We've gotten really good at shutting out what we hear. As a result, we no longer know how to listen.

What Is Listening?

Listening is not identifying sounds. It is the art of paying attention to someone else. Yes, we are back to getting that pronoun "I" out of our thoughts and out as the primary focus of our communication. How often do you find yourself in a situation where someone is telling you something about an issue that matters to them—and you are busy doing something else at the same time? You may excuse what you are doing as multitasking. But what you're doing is avoiding listening. You're still in your I box, doing what you want to do, and relegating the other person to the background. That is not paying attention to someone else; it's feeding your own ego about how great you are that you are "listening" but also doing what you want to do.

Now imagine that same scenario. But imagine instead of looking at your email, adjusting papers on your desk, checking your smart phone, cooking dinner, or whatever, that you stop, turn, and face the person. Watch his face. Watch the emotions that accompany the words. Really aim to focus 100 percent if possible on his words. Just imagine for a moment what would happen if you did give this person all the attention you could. If you really listened to what he had to say? What will happen if you take those two minutes to contemplate the other person?

Contemplation of the other is crucial. As one of my colleagues states, all of us carry around an invisible sign around our necks that says, "Please notice me." Imagine how paying attention would change the look on someone's face—the one who was trying to tell you something yesterday or even a day before. It could be a coworker, a spouse, or a child. Think of what would've happened had you really paid attention; what would have happened if you truly listened. How would the other person have reacted?

When we hear about paying attention to the other person and listening, immediately many of us start thinking about all of the studies we have read about how poor modern-day listening skills are. All those studies do is depress us. Listening can be easy. All you have to do is approach it in a Zen way. What do I mean by that? Well, first, as I keep repeating, get the I out. Focus on the other person; hear her words.

Most of us don't listen because we're really waiting for our turn to speak. Think about it: we may hear the other person's words but immediately go into a defense of our own positions, a comment on the positions or one about why we think what we think, or just about anything else that is self-centered. In Zen, we aim for no emotional reactions—and all of these are emotional reactions. Try ignoring the focus on out-talking the other person and instead listen to what he has to say. Doing so can be very easy. Whenever your own thoughts or your own reactions of "Yes, but I need to say this" appears in your mind, do something physical to stop them.

How? You can try something simple such as sitting on your hands; for many, having their hands contained keeps them from talking. Free hands equal free speech. Contained hands equal listening. Having a rubber band around your wrist that you pop whenever the "I" thoughts intrude also can be effective. Whatever you use, the main intent is to keep you focused on the other person, not on your own internal need to speak.

We don't even have to recognize all the words the person is saying. Some of us also tend to let our inner English teacher take over when we attempt to listen, correcting grammar, ideas or even adding prompts for the speaker, trying to hurry them to finish. Both tactics are more I-centered behavior. Instead, just hear the words. In one famous Zen koan, the master instructs the pupil to be like a stone in a river and stay still, letting the water flow about him. Apply that concept to listening: let the words flow. No action is necessary—but observation and acknowledgment is.

All we really need to do is concentrate on the other person. Take time and distance from your own emotions to observe the emotion of the speaker. How does this person feel about what he is saying? Look at the face. Observe how it reacts and moves with the words. Look at the body language. You don't need to interpret or judge; just observe. By doing so, you will find yourself with a much deeper and better understanding of the person's ideas.

Now you may also be saying to me, "I communicate with this person always through the web. I've never heard his voice." Perhaps. Yet the same ideas apply. Most of us don't read emails or web-based documents; we scan them. We also tend to scan them with that same waiting-for-the-chance-to-respond mindset rather than absorbing the message. Our intent becomes to check off the email and get the message off our plate so we can be on to something we want to do. So we react. "He wants what by when? He's got to be mental." Or "How many times is he going to ask me that same question?" or even "Why do they send me this junk?" Yes, maybe he does want it by an unrealistic time—but maybe he's given you all the notice he himself was given. Maybe there's a bigger, newer need. Or yes, maybe he is self-centered and can't plan.

None of that matters. Taking the Zen approach to such documents helps here as well. For instance, instead of scanning or approaching the email with an I approach, take a moment just to read the message and observe one of the emotions at work in it. You may feel empathy. You may be surprised at what you hear that is NOT said.

Again, no judgment. No reaction. Be the rock in the river. Just observe.

When you judge, you let your I focus get into the other person's ideas and message. As a result, you do not get the entire value of understanding the other person. Remember that understanding the audience is the critical point of all communication; if all you're thinking about is yourself and your reactions, you've missed the point. Just observe it, then take that information, write it down, or put it somewhere in your head. I'm not asking you to do anything with that information. Just be aware of it. Just observe. Just as Zen tells you to observe what is going on around you, and by observing you will be ready to understand the world, observing the other person will help ensure that you'll be ready to write or communicate with this person. Observing may also give you a much bigger picture than you would have if all you did was react and scan.

Why is she asking you the same question? Well, possibly she didn't read your answer the first time. Or maybe she forgot. Or maybe, just maybe, you didn't answer well. Perhaps your answer was unclear if you answered in a hurry with your mind on something else. Or perhaps what she really wants to know is something bigger and she either doesn't know how to put that in words—or perhaps isn't quite aware of it herself. Observing will allow you to see those needs, that bigger picture.

How does good listening help you determine who the audience is? If you understand the emotions, the points, the words, and the ideas from the other person, you're going to understand what makes that person function. And you will begin to understand how you can build a relationship with that person.

Relationship?

You may be saying, "Why would I want to build a relationship with this person? I'm merely asking for a refund for product or asking for help." All of life is symbiotic.

Many of us stare into our devices, laptops, tablets, and phones and become so focused on the narcissistic quality of ourselves we fail to see how much we really need other people. And once we recognize that fact, listen to the other person, and are aware of who she is, we are one giant step forward on the path to Zen communication.

CHAPTER 6

Honor the Structure

In the beginner's mind are many possibilities, but in the expert's mind there are few.[1]

—Shunrye Suzuki, Zen master

Now that you have identified your goals and your audience, it's time to decide how to structure your message. Structure is vital to communication. How you form your message is much the same as how energy is formed into matter: an idea occurs, and then that energy is shaped in an appropriate way for the intent to take shape.

Everything in nature has structure. Even an atom has a structure, as you may remember from chemistry class: various ions revolve around the nucleus. What may appear as random in nature will reveal its structure upon closer inspection. Even modern poetry has structure, although that structure may also be unapparent.

Only human behavior can be random and unstructured, but as Zen teaches us, lack of structure and simplicity leads to chaos.

Which is why good business communication also has to have structure. Back in the Dark Ages, when we all did business exclusively by phone, we had an accepted protocol and structure: instead of immediately barking our request when the other party answered the phone, we said hello and identified ourselves. We then set the stage for what we were about to ask. Now that we communicate electronically most of the time, we often forget structure. As we have discussed, we hunker down in our own stuff, intent on getting out the message as fast as we can.

---

[1] EXT_ONLY

Think for a moment: how do you act when you open an email and see a big dense paragraph with long strings of sentences? Do you want to read it? Most people don't. In fact, most people don't read it. The communication isn't successful; instead, it's an amorphous big black blob of verbiage, full of the writer's intent to get the message off his plate and totally missing any attempt to shape it into a message that can be understood.

But what shape does one use to communicate? That depends on the message.

Remember that argument that all communication is persuasive in nature? Although many will argue with this opinion, in actuality this argument makes a lot of sense. Think for a moment: even in a statement such as "it's a pretty day outside" you are persuading the other person to see your point of view or to enter a conversation with you. Whether you agree with the persuasive intent of all communication, one fact remains: all communication is about getting the other person to see the product of your mind. So shaping the message in a manner that will be easiest for the receiver to perceive is the best way to make sure that your message is successful.

In Zen, one intends to harness the energy of two opposing forces to create harmony. This concept is very similar to what you do when you structure a message. Before you structure, you will (hopefully) have analyzed what your goal of the message is to be; by doing so, what you have done is shape your thought into form. That form is now your energy of thought. You have also analyzed the audience in detail; you know as much as possible about the other person's thoughts, attitudes, and knowledge. Perhaps you also have an idea of how this person will structure his own energy and response. You know his mindset, and you know the environment in which she is working. You now have a sense of her energy. That becomes the energy of perception in which your message will operate.

So when you structure the message, what you are doing is indeed making peace with these two opposing forces. Some messages are more opposing than are others; each message will be different, even if they go to the same person. Yet you still have more than one form of energy out of which to make one united and connected thought between you, the sender, and the receiver. This, my friends, is the essence of Zen in business.

When you are helping the other person see why your energy of thought is important and why it is worthy of attention, you connect.

But it's not just a casual fly-by connection; by using the appropriate structure for the message, you connect more deeply. The bond strengthens. And with that strengthened bond, action occurs. Action leads to interaction, which leads to opportunities for both parties.

But what if the receiver of the message misses the beauty of the united thought? Then you have to take a step back and re-examine the structure. Often what is important to you isn't immediately important to the other person. In fact, most of the time, what's immediately apparent and important to us is not as clear to the other person. That's why good business writing use a technique called the WIFM.

The WIFM—or What's in It for Me?

Someone once said we all have a very favorite radio station playing in our heads: station WIFM—what's in it for me? (Note the acronym neatly bypasses the double I. Think about that. Less I than we think necessary.) This acronym is a standard one in business communication circles; it's a short way of saying that most people live in a self-centered world. Our thoughts are our reality—and usually our thoughts are about ourselves. So when you open and scan your email, the first thing you look for is a message that matters to you—what's in it for me. As you read it, you may be thinking, "Ok, yada yada; so what's in this for me? Why did you send this to me?" (Be honest; we all read our emails this way most of the time.)

My favorite way of understanding the WIFM comes from my friend Merrilyn the psychotherapist (the *psycho*-therapist, as she calls herself). Her statement is that as we grow and age, we still keep the kernels of who we were inside us—sort of like a tree growing new rings each year. Now, based on Merrilyn's statement, here's my explanation of the WIFM. Deep down inside each of us lives the three-year-old, who has no concept of time and can be distracted in a heartbeat; the five-year-old who drives everyone crazy with the *why* questions and who just doesn't seem to get it as fast as the older kids; the seven-year-old who chatters incessantly; the thirteen-year-old who barely speaks to you at all.

Depending on the day you are having, one of these earlier versions of yourself may take center stage and direct your actions. So if I'm having a stressful day, the five-year-old and the seven-year-old may duke it out to see who controls the public me—and the people who communicate with me need to know that my inner kids are asking, "Hey! Do I have to? What did you say again? How come I have to listen? Does this mean that if I listen now you will let me go watch TV and veg? I don't want to hear what you have to say; I want to tell you about what I want to talk about" and so on. Or more likely I might be pushed and having a day where my inner teenager comes out. I may be inwardly snarly and say, "Oh, yeah? Says who? Make me care. If not, I'll just ignore you and do whatever I want to do."

As the communicator, you never know which of these multiple personalities will emerge in your audience. So you spend a little time thinking about the person you are communicating with. Why should she care? Have you made your point so clear that she can't be distracted? Have you allowed her to talk a little as well? Acknowledging and honoring the WIFM allows you to have good manners, so to speak. You let the other person's needs and interests go first. But she then usually has good manners in return: once you have acknowledged her and her interests, she is willing to listen to yours.

That's the WIFM. Now if you take the lessons of the WIFM as you craft your message, you'll realize that what you really have to do is catch the attention of the other person. Many of us read or listen, as we have discussed, with our minds on autopilot. You have to catch that person's attention quickly with the answer to "what's in it for me?"

Think of structuring your message this way: imagine the person sitting in front of the computer with a remote control in his hand, just the same way many people sit in front of a TV with the remote. He starts clicking away until something startles him into consciousness. Whatever has grabbed him has answered "Hey, this is something for you!" and he pays attention. His energy of perception merges with your energy of thought, and a clear message occurs. That's what you want in your structure. You want him to notice your words. (See how the idea of all communication being persuasive plays out here?)

OK, but How Do You Do It?

What you have to use is what I refer to as *USA Today* writing: you get the headline up front. When you craft your message, your most important sentence answers that WIFM. That's the line that becomes the very first sentence.

Many of us have been taught to build a paragraph in the deductive inverted pyramid style. We start from the broad and we narrow to the point, which usually comes at the end of the paragraph. Although this process works very well for long in-depth papers or reports or proposals, it is deadly for business communication; most of us not only don't have the time to read someone else's deduction but we also don't want to. We want what we need to know now—and fast.

The inverted pyramid, therefore, doesn't work to catch someone's attention. It starts too broadly, allowing that person far too much space to wander mentally and get off the path. Now, if you flip that paragraph and begin with headline up front, you catch the person's attention. You answer the WIFM and also set the tone. You also signal how you will structure that harmony out of the two opposing points of energy and thoughts.

Years ago *USA Today* had a billboard ad campaign about the usefulness of its abbreviated, get-to-the-point style of reporting. One of the billboards read "Pigs house destroyed; huffing and puffing suspected." Although humorous, the billboard was nevertheless extremely successful. Not only did it send the message that you could get all you needed to know from one short article, but it also answered the WIFM for reading a different type of newspaper. What was in it for us was all the basics we needed to know in two short sentences—a style that has become the hallmark for many online newspapers and websites.

Let's take a look at an example of how structure changes response and unity. Consider the two emails that follow, both about the same idea, with the same goal and the same audience. Which one works better to create action?

> Email A:
> Subject: Useful tool to help you edit your papers
> Dear class,
> I have noticed that many of you are struggling to focus your thesis in the most efficient direction. As a result, you may be frustrated at not being able to find research to back up your points. You may also be frustrated at not being able to work at a pace you'd prefer on this paper. To help you, I've listed some free websites below to help you with that thesis.

Boring, isn't it? Why? It has a WIFM. It has a goal. It has analyzed the audience's needs. What it lacks—and what makes it boring—is lack of effective structure.

Let's look at a revised version.

> Email B:
> Subject: Want an A on your paper?
> An A paper always starts with a great thesis statement.
> A great thesis statement will make a paper easier and faster to write, Spending a little time on focusing the thesis will save you time by giving you structure, research direction, the necessary details you'll need—as well as save you time.
> Wondering if your thesis could stand some tweaking? Try one of the free websites listed below.
> A strong paper with a strong thesis is always easier for me to grade—and usually results in a more successful grade. We both win!
> What are you waiting for? Try the websites!

Notice how this one grabs the reader? Yes, it sounds a lot like the RonCo products ads we see on TV. Yet here's the secret: these ads work.

Basically, now that you have an idea that everything is persuasive, setting up your message couldn't be simpler. Just as all of nature has patterns, such as how rocks, trees, and other natural items appear always in an odd number, patterning your message is very easy. First you know you have to grab the reader's attention. That means the headline has to go up first, followed up immediately by the WIFM in the same sentence if possible. If not, the second sentence should answer the WFIM.

So now you have a clear view of your first section of the persuasive message. Now what? You answer the 5 W's.

The 5 W's: Six Words That Can Change Your Life

"The next meeting of the budget committee will be held on Friday at 2. Please plan to be there."

—faulty email

Ever received an email that required you to reply asking for clarification? How about a voice mail that led to your playing telephone tag to figure out what the caller wanted? If you're like most people, your answer may be "Yes—most of my email is like that!" How do you feel about those emails? If you are like most people, the answer is *resentful.* Instead of being able to answer and get on with your work, you have to wait and clarify, and then maybe clarify again, before you can get this issue off your plate.

Does the sender mean to be self-absorbed? Probably not. Most likely she is unaware that she hasn't been complete and that is she has piled more on your to-do list. And she could have avoided doing so by being aware of a simple formula called the 5 W's: *who, what, when, where, why,* and *how.* Although the answer to *how* is important and is usually included in this basic formula, the originators of this technique named it the 5 W's and left out the H. The H is often one of the most important questions you can ask. So we will include it as part of the acronym.

The 5 W's are usually thought of as a journalism technique. Yet they are invaluable and necessary in business. Asking yourself if you have answered all these questions before you hit "Send" or leave that message can ensure that you have given the recipient all he needs to act on your message.

Here's how you think about crafting your message; ask yourself the following questions:

1. *Who*—who am I talking about?
2. *What*—what exactly do I mean here? Have I specified what exactly I need you to do? How about what is involved? Have I clarified all steps?
3. *When*—did I give complete date and time information?
4. *Where*—do I need to clarify any location so the reader has no questions?
5. *Why*—have I told why the requested information or action is important? The more I specify, the better the results.
6. *How*—how are we going to accomplish what we need to do?

Now let's go back and look at our example about the budget committee meeting.

Who: Perhaps you are on the budget committee and the *who* seems self-evident. But perhaps on this week's agenda the group is discussing upgrades to IT. Most likely you realize that the director of IT also needs to be there. But if you think through the entire message, we may find we need to add some other players.

What: What is exactly on the agenda this week? What's the point of the meeting? Maybe I have a huge project due; without any further information, I may decide this meeting is one I can skip. But if I don't know what the meeting is about, how can I make that decision? (Note: many emails such as this one will have an agenda attached. Well and good—but the highlights of the agenda need to be in the email body itself. Otherwise the sender is infringing on my time, asking me to open the attachment each time I need to refer to the reminder of the meeting.)

When: Yes, I know the meeting starts at 2. But how long is it going to last? I have another meeting at 3. Can I make them both?

Where: Hey, what room are we meeting in?

Why: Well, yes, that is the point. Are we meeting just to meet? What is this particular meeting supposed to achieve? [See the *what* above.] If I don't know, I may just show up. But if I then find out that we are meeting to discuss IT, and perhaps decide what upgrades we need to the software, I can come prepared and be able to contribute more to the discussion. And if we are going to discuss upgrades, maybe we need to ask not only the director of IT but some of the users. They should know exactly what they need and perhaps save us time and money. [See *who* above.]

How—are we going to come away from this meeting with a plan and recommendation or are we going to be given tasks? What's up?

Now you may be thinking, "Who has time to write—much less read—all that?" Correct. No one does. But you do have time to think all that; doing so may take at most a minute. Then you can craft the answers to these questions in almost as short an email:

> *The budget committee will meet this Friday from 2–3 in the board room. Since the goal of this meeting is to create a list of recommended software upgrades, the director of IT will join us. Come prepared with research, suggestions, and a calculator. If you can think of anyone whose expertise we need at this meeting, please let me know.*

See how having answered the 5 W's makes the whole message clearer? And how the recipient now knows exactly what is expected of her—and that she can make her 3:00 meeting?

Many business people complain that they simply don't have the time to write well. Actually, the converse is true: they don't have the time *not* to write well.

Why? Well, to start with, each time someone sends out a poorly written email or leaves an obtuse voice mail, he has in effect asked the receiver of the communication to figure out what he meant by the message. Instead of the reader being able to understand immediately what the writer meant, she has to stop and take time to decipher possibilities. In other words, the self-absorbed sender has wasted the receiver's time. The receiver then retaliates by having to ask questions, which leads to putting more work on the sender's plate. Or she just ignores the whole issue, grinding productivity to a halt. What could have been a 2-minute job expands to hours while each one waits for clarification.

By answering the 5 W's before you communicate, you'll see your time expand, your productivity increase, and your colleagues more willing to work with you. These six words can change your life.

What Else Do I Need to Think About?

Have you ever read something and thought, "Well, that's all well and good; what do you want me to do about it?" If you have, the writer fell victim to assuming that you knew what she wanted you to do. Very few of us can read minds. That's why telling the reader what action you want from him is so important. This section should complete your basic persuasive structure.

Although what you want from the reader may be obvious to you, it rarely is obvious to the reader unless you tell him. When you write, you see all of the details inside the bits and nuances that went into your message. You see the supporting details that lead you to ask for him to take this action. But the reader is presented with a wide screenshot of a large picture, and unless you tell him what part to focus on and where to go to next, he will continue to stay here wondering what's in this for him. Make what you want him to do clear—and make the action easy.

To do so, you'll need to put yourself back in those reader's shoes. Imagine yourself, sitting there, having read the message. Now what? What is it that you want him to do? Think step by step, as if you are controlling the person like a robot and you the driver inside.

Observe every clear, tiny step. That observation, part of this Zen mantra of keeping things broken into simple parts, is crucial.

All of us like simple, easy-to-do actions. If you tell the reader step-by-step what you want, you're more likely to get it. Think about all of those direct mail messages. Many of them ask you to "pick up the phone and give us a call." They flash the phone number in front of you, removing all excuses for not complying.

Give the reader clear and easy actions in just the same way. If you tell the person to gather information and send the report back to you by Friday, you really aren't giving clear directions. But if you say, "Call finance for data, call Sally in accounting for paid to date information, and look at last year's sales reports to see what our gross projections were compared against our actual sales," you've told him not only what to do but more importantly what you want and how to do it.

In Zen, actions cause reactions. Remember that you're harnessing opposing forces of energy. Here one force of energy is your intent. The other is the receiver's interpretation. By aligning that energy with what you want, you are much more likely to create a peaceful unity. By that, I mean that you will get the answer to your question or request, just as you wanted, and the other person will have satisfaction and peace in knowing he gave you just what you wanted.

This Sounds Like an Outline

Well, yes, it is. Hold on—don't shut the book just yet.

Many people make the mistake of thinking that once they have their goal and have identified their audience, they're ready to write. They run and jump up and down like SpongeBob, yelling, "I'm ready! I'm ready!" Yet they wind up being just as foolish as he is. While enthusiasm is great, nothing good comes from thoughtless enthusiasm—at least not in a Zen approach to business writing.

If you're rushing to write, you're still thinking in that "I" focus mentality. Your mind is so full of what you want to occur and what you want the audience to do that you are still thinking of the reader as a mirror of yourself. You may in reality be so ready to get the message off your plate that you tire yourself with possibilities. You see all kinds of bright possibilities, all kinds of great reactions to your message, and you're ready to rock. But keeping the focus on the present involves making sure that you take a few more steps to ensure that the journey is successful.

Remember that the successful journey has to pay deliberate attention to each one of the steps. You're not ready to write just because you have your goal and have identified your audience. Now instead you need to bring order out of chaos. Just because you see all the details associated with the ideas and the message that you want to send doesn't mean your reader does. The reader has a separate mind; therefore he has no idea how to bring order out of your chaos. You see the logical connections; you see the details—but he does not. You have to show him.

That's where your next step must take you: to create an effective, orderly piece of communication, you have to have an outline. Yes, I know.

I just saw that cringe at the word *outline.* An outline, however, is no more than a list—a quick way to ensure you haven't forgotten anything and you have indeed taken a look at all of those 5 W's that we talked about before.

An outline helps you organize your thoughts. A good outline can also save you tons of time; doing your thinking before you write ensures that the first draft is better than what might be your sixth draft without one. It becomes a roadmap, for both you and the reader, and it allows you to write in stop and starts: it allows you to stop and take a Dairy Queen break or even leave the document alone for a while without worrying that the idea will run off and leave you. And when you return, you know where you are going and what you want to do next. That trusty outline will have you on the path to your goal in no time.

Creating an outline doesn't have to be difficult. It doesn't even have to be in full sentences. In fact, one of my favorite ways to approach an outline—and one that is a great example of Zen thinking—is to keep it really simple. I do so by keeping my outline on a two-inch square post-it note. For most of my communication, that's all I need. Why a two-inch square post-it note, you ask? To keep me honest.

In simplicity is beauty—but simplicity is hard.

We don't want to do the work to keep things simple; chaos is easy to wallow in—and easy to use to shift the blame elsewhere when our thinking isn't the best. But to distill the essence of my goal, my message and my details to fit clearly on that two-inch square, I have to jettison the junk that keeps me getting in my own way. I have to think about what really matters and why, which means I have to think about the other person, not just myself.

Using this post-it note outline technique is also simple. I start with writing "goal" at the top and then list *audience, benefits, who, what, when, where, why, how do I know?* (And you thought the technique would be hard.) Then I go back and fill in the answers. There; I have an outline.

Next comes the magic step, and I do mean it is magic: I post that post-it note on the right top of my computer screen. In fact, I used to have a computer that let me create the post-it note as part of my screen and move it where I wanted it—that is, move it anywhere as long as I could check off that I had finished the task. Talk about a discipline motivator! Every email or online story I found interesting still had that post-it dangling in front of me, reminding that I needed to stay on my path. By having that note in front of you, you can't veer off into unimportant details; the inner critic in you won't let you.

Maybe. How Do I Use It to Create Structure? And What's in It for Me, Anyhow?

With the idea of headline up front, you are already started on structure. Having the 5 W's and the Call to Action also help. But the best thing that having structure—yes, an outline—can do for you, the writer, is make the job simpler to do. Humans like simplicity. They may also like decorations on that simplicity, as in chocolate syrup on ice cream, but the decorations that succeed are simple. You'll note that the best details are those that continue a basic simple structure.

> We like white space. In Zen, this concept is called clear space, or time for clarity.

When the space in front of us is empty, we can examine what is around it in context. By having each piece listed out, we know what needs to go there. Written communication is no different: we like our white space. We like our concepts—in short, easy-to-read paragraphs. So knowing that, we now arrange the ideas around the white space. We have paint-by-numbers. We have a map. We can take one step at a time, take it simply, and we are suddenly done.

So What Do I Do?

Everything starts with the beginning. So the first paragraph has to start with the headline up in the first sentence. It then ends with a transition sentence that tells the point of the writing—the WIFM. And no more. So in your outline, you listed the goal, the 5 W's, and the WIFM. Write them in sentence format and you now have a paragraph. Note that a transition sentence may be an elaboration on the why in the first sentence. It may be an elaboration on the how. But it tells the basics and the WIFM and no more.

You've already completed a good third of the job. That paragraph, by the way, may be all you need. Depending on intent of your message, and expectation of the audience, that nitty gritty may be all that you need. How to tell? Ask yourself if the reader needs anything else to succeed. If not—and you have truly put yourself in your reader's shoes, without expecting him to have all the knowledge of the situation you do—you don't need any more. As a colleague once observed, good writing should be like a mini-skirt: long enough to cover what's important but short enough to be interesting.

But let's say your recipient needs more. You then move on to more structure—the next part of the outline. You begin a new paragraph. Why? Because you are moving to a new idea. New idea, or new focus on the previous idea, means new paragraph. We need to see items and information in their white space; doing so allows us clarity.

If you need it, the second paragraph details how. Give the reader the information he needs to be successful here—you will have new 5 W's. Write those down. Make them into sentences. Make the paragraph clear and concise and make it concrete—but don't let it go over five typed lines.

Why? By limiting yourself, you stay in the "what does the reader need to know" focus and discipline yourself from wallowing in the "here's the clutter of my brain" abyss. Moreover, sticking to the five typed lines helps you simplify, getting back to that nitty gritty before you shoot yourself in the foot. And finally, by keeping the paragraph short, you add to the white space not only on the page, but in the reader's mind—and in your mind as you write.

If you have steps or lots of details in this paragraph, use bullets or enumeration in this paragraph. That creates a map within the document, again for the ease of both the reader to follow but also for you to think through. (It also makes the details easier to write.)

So once you have completed that paragraph, are you done? Can you hit Send and let the message go merrily in its way? No. Nothing in nature occurs in even numbers. And that law of physics, whether we are aware of it or not, leaves us feeling imbalance with just two paragraphs. To leave the reader feeling as if the message is complete, you need at least a third paragraph. (Sometimes you need to break up that middle section into two or more paragraphs. If it begins to look cluttered, remember white space. Find a spot in it where the idea shifts just a bit, put your cursor there, and hit Enter. Voila! Instant white space. Easier to read document. Better writing. And with very little effort.)

This last paragraph is your call to action. It may be something as simple as thanking the reader and telling him how to reach you if he needs more. It can include one or two directions. But it has to be short. Honor the clarity and honor the outline.

This three-part outline will work for most communications that need more than just the quick facts. It works for emails. It works for written hard documents, such as letters confirming details or delivering good news. It even works as the template for longer documents, such as basic reports. In place of an opening sentence that details the 5 W'S, you'll have an opening section that sets out all the 5 W'S. Included in that section, at the end, will be the WIFM, or thesis, that tells the reader exactly what point this document will provide. The second section will lay out the details, and the third will state in clear and detailed format what call to action the report has identified.

Will This Structure Always Work?

Most of the time, if you are just offering information that has no emotional baggage attached. Other types of messages require different structure. Delivering bad news, for instance, requires more details simply because someone's emotions are involved.

As Carl Rogers, the father of industrial psychology, acknowledged, to communicate well, we have to empathize. When we receive news that is contrary to what we had hoped it would be, we usually want to know more about why. Therefore, in a bad-news message, we write using a structure that helps answer that why.

- We start again with the same opening paragraph.
- The second paragraph gives the factors that lead to the bad news or decision. Think of this paragraph as setting out the individual facts and items, each in its own clarity and wholeness. By doing so you create a buffer from having the news or decision be met with emotion, not reason.
- The third paragraph then relates the bad news.

- The fourth paragraph then gives follow up, encouragement, or alternatives. By doing so, we show that empathy that Rogers said was so important. We also stress why the decision is as it is.

In this structure, we put the bad news in a sandwich. Why? Because we need to be able to contemplate the message without emotion, and putting it between buffers help us see not only the knee-jerk bad news but also alternatives and hope.

Structure Works

Yes. All life is matter in structured form. Why should communication be any different?

CHAPTER 7

Honor Clarity

The beginning is the most important part of the work.
— Plato, *The Republic*

The worst part of most documents is the beginning. That's really unfortunate because the beginning, or the first few minutes, of any document is where the reader forms her opinion of whether the writer's idea, or the writer, is any good. In other words, it's one of the most important parts of any document, not only to the document's success but to your own career.

Most really mediocre (or really rotten) beginnings come not from a lack of effort, but a lack of knowledge of how to start. As my friend Stuart says, the mere thought of having to start melds with the thought of having to do the whole thing, which melds with the thought of having someone judge the whole thing, and instead of starting you'd much rather go back to bed and hide under the covers.

Work usually doesn't let us do that, not even if we work from home. So armed with all those old sayings such as "the journey of a thousand miles begins with a single step," we grit our teeth and dive in. Note that I said *dive in*. Think for a moment here: to dive in, one has to have a pool of deep water—either that, or risk a broken neck. We *see* that deep water, lots and lots and lots of it, and the whole, the entirety, surrounds us. We dive in, deeper and down, and struggle in the enormity of coming to the top.

That's how most of us start to write. We dive in and struggle to the surface, and only then we see where we are going. And in writing, by then, we think we are usually somewhere well on what we think is our way to having the whole thing over—the metaphorical other side of the pool. The effort to get to the surface to make progress, however, exhausts us. We wind up with so little energy or strength that we barely can thrash our way to the finish.

But let's think through this process. Let's look at the Michael Phelps school of diving in as a way to start our writing. When kids are taught to swim and dive properly, they know that *down* is not an option. Going deep and having to surface takes an enormous amount of energy. When we go down, we have to use all our strength just to get back up—and once we do, most of us have no idea where we are.

Good swimmers know that the goal isn't down. It's out—it's as far toward the middle of the pool as possible. Take a look at some of those online videos of Phelps competing at the Olympics. Watch his stance on the stand, way before he hits the water. He isn't looking down at all; he's looking out—out to his goal, which is the other side of the pool, even when he has to flip and return to the starting blocks. He's already planning just how to manage his energy to get there in truly record time. And when he hits the water, he literally hits the water: he barely goes under. Instead he keeps to the essentials and moves forward. For Phelps, the essentials are the point—the goal—and the bare bones basics of what will get him there.

To put this in writing terms, take a look at the following email:

> Harvey,
> I was wondering if you went to the meeting last week, the one where Jim and Todd explained the new marketing plan? Well, I wondered that if you did, perhaps you took notes? And if you did, could I look at them? I wasn't there and I really need to know if I missed anything that I will need to know tomorrow when I talk with Our Client.
> Thank you in advance!
> Larry

Hear the struggle? Poor old Larry is a thrasher, in deep and wasting all of Harvey's good will and attention by trying to get to the point. And he's put so much effort and words into trying to get to the other side of the message that he loses it along the way.

Compare it to this version:

> Harvey,
> Do you have any notes from last week's marketing meeting that I
> might want to review before I meet with Our Client tomorrow?
> Thanks!
> Jonathan

Jonathan obviously falls in the Phelps school of starting. What he's done is thought of where he wants to go with this message. What does he want Harvey to know? What does he need from Harvey? Why?

And he's asked it. He's asked just that—and no more. That's clarity. Let's explore some ideas than can help you develop the clarity you need in your writing.

Watch Your Paragraphing

No matter what you may remember from high school, a good paragraph is one that is easy to read. People can take only so much at a time. Think of your paragraph as a picture: your reader is able see only so much detail at once. No one has enough time to look long and hard, as if she were hunting for Waldo in a *Where's Waldo?* book. So the rule is one idea equals one sentence. One group of sentences that explore that same idea equals one paragraph. However, no matter what, you can't see all the details at one glance or the whole Waldo scene. You have to start with one focal point. In writing, that one focal point equals one idea. But perhaps you're not clear on exactly what is one idea. Think of it in this way: how much can you take in with that one quick glance? The answer will become one sentence. One idea equals one sentence.

You'll need more than one sentence, however, to develop that idea; those sentences come together to create a developed idea in what is known as a paragraph. Maybe you need six glances, or six sentences, to flesh out those ideas into a cohesive paragraph. So how long should a paragraph be? Ask six English teachers and you will get six different answers. Usually the answer is something along the lines of "topic, support, and transition"—which tells you virtually nothing useful—or "as long as it takes to cover the subject."

That last answer is also vague. We're looking for clarity. Therefore, we need clear guidelines, no vague possibilities. One interesting and helpful way to approach clarity is by examining how the human brain works. If we can take in only so much as a time, can we quantify that "so much"?

Blake and Bly, in their classic take on E.B. White's *Elements of Style,* called *Elements of Business Writing (1991),* offered the following salvo:

> *The problem with today's business writing is not that it is too simple but that it blithely ignores or exhausts the reader. Experienced writers understand that even sophisticated readers like a break from polysyllabic words, long sentences, endless footnotes, and writing aimed at showing off* (p. 7)

Blake and Bly also note that "readers rebel against large chunks of type. They absorb information more easily when it is presented in short, coherent units" (p. 10).

So let's go back to that idea of paragraphing as taking a picture. Look around for a moment and find one object. It can be your coffee cup, your pet cat, or your signed Willie Mays baseball. That object becomes your *subject*—the thing you are going to show me a picture of. Now hold your hands up in front of you, fingers spread and thumbs touching, with the palms of your hands facing outward. You'll now have the stereotypical gesture that entertainment uses to make fun of photographers and film-makers. Take those touching thumbs and gesture and focus them on your object. That's one picture.

Now shift your body slightly to the right, keeping your hands still in front of you. You now have a new picture. Same subject, but a different focus on the subject. Now translate: one picture equals one paragraph. Shift in focus equals a new picture, or new paragraph.

Now think about focus. If you pull too far away from your subject, you will have lots of background items in your picture of the subject. In fact, you will have so much that the reader will be distracted, or have to spend lots of time understanding what exactly your subject is. A non-focused or too-large paragraph will have the same effect; your readers will most likely miss your point. But if you focus in on the subject, you find the details of it. You have plenty to focus on, but now the reader knows what your subject is and can concentrate on how your communication here delivers your message.

Focus gives clarity. Clarity means order. And order means a simple decluttering of ideas.

But how does one do that? A good litmus test here is that a clear paragraph can be no longer than 12 tight lines. Note that I said tight *lines*; I did not say typed *sentences*. The way to test is very easy: you simply look at your paragraph, go to the left-hand margin, and begin to count the number of typed lines. You may have 16 lines, you may have 4, or, if you are like many people who work in abstractions, you may have 30.

Now count again. With a pencil if you have a hard copy, or with the highlight feature in your word processor, set off the 9th through 14th line. Now read the copy just in that section. What you most likely will find is somewhere between the 10th and the 12th line you will have shifted thought. You will have a word such as *and*, a phrase such as *in this case*, or some other transitional device. In other words, your mind will have already shifted focus. Your mind unconsciously will have rearranged the thought. No matter how much your conscious mind and your decisions try to get in the way, the unconscious mind has an idea of when it has reached overload.

Electronic communication requires that we use even fewer lines per block of prose. We take in less when we see a picture or document on a screen; here the litmus test is that an electronic paragraph should contain no more than six typed lines. Otherwise, the reader can't grasp the meaning in that one quick read.

So what do you do? Your unconscious and the natural order of Zen in the world has edited for you. Put your cursor where the focus of idea shifts, hit Enter, and voila! You have a more readable document. This is not the proverbial brain surgery. Remember that old saying that the journey of 1000 miles begins with one step? It sounds corny, but it is true. Hitting the enter key where your unconscious told you to shift is one of those very simple steps that takes you on the journey to clarity. If you do nothing else but this little technique, you have increased the readability of your document—and made it simpler.

To get anything done, you have to imagine each step of the journey. That is why you have to focus in an enlarger reality screen and take a quick and hard look at exactly all the details you are sending. Only in that way can you get the results you want—and also build a positive relationship with your reader.

Create a Map

By breaking down the paragraphs visually, you have already started to create clarity. You have started sorting the chaos and looking at the individual pieces. This concept is Zen-based; it is all about seeing the small things as parts of the whole.

Now that you have two separate paragraphs or perhaps three, you can then start looking for the main idea in each one of the paragraphs. Just as you started by stating the main idea and what's in it for the reader in the opening of the entire document, you now look and see if each one of the paragraphs has the main idea upfront.

You look at the entire paragraph just as you would look at the overall document. What's the goal of the paragraph? Have I made it clear what I want the reader to do? Have I filled it with clutter? That last question is a vital question.

Zen asks that we reduce to the simplest all things that are in our lives. By reducing to simplicity, we make logical connections and increase clarity.

So because you had your writing broken into manageable pieces, the logical next step is to make it more focused. We've already talked about focusing your idea; now we want to focus on making things clear. Ever looked at a map or a document on your phone and had to make it larger so that you could see the details? You had to focus and to see the details. That's exactly what you need to do now. You need to break the idea into small manageable pieces, just as you would break down any task.

Be Specific

Think for moment. We all have this big panoramic view going on in our heads, and while we hope we know what each part means, it's the simple steps that make things successful. If I tell you, for instance, that I'd like you to stop and buy some flowers on the way home, I'm opening up a great deal of possibility.

Although a request such as this seems to be pretty simple, clear, and direct, it is not. Asking someone to stop by the store on his way home may mean to you stopping at the local grocery store; for others, that interpretation may be different. My husband, for example, would wind up calling me and asking me if getting flowers from a particular location would be okay—or did I have a specialty florist in mind when I made that request? He's a details person, one who wants to know and make sure that every small detail is correct. Although seems obvious to you, adding the small detail of naming the store is a simple way to add more clarity to the other person's mind.

And what about "buy some flowers"? In your mind you may need a bunch of the bright fresh spring flowers that Trader Joe's has in abundance for $3.99. But in someone else's mind, flowers could mean something else entirely. The other person may bring home some artificially blue and kind of dead-looking flowers simply because you didn't specify. And my daughter's kind-hearted and free-spirited friend Harvey would have bought the flowers, but she would have given them away to people who looked as if they needed cheering up before she ever got home. Her reason? You told me to buy flowers. You didn't say what to do with them.

You also may mean a small bunch of regular flowers that don't cost much, yet again what's in your mind isn't necessarily what is in the other person's. He could bring home a dozen roses, which, while nice, may break your grocery budget. You could wind up with a potted plant, which in the purchaser's mind still falls under the category of flowers. Although all of these are nice options, they are not necessarily what you want.

Words have specific power. For example, ask six people you know to describe a sports car. Give them no other information other than "tell me what a sports car looks like." One person will equate *sports car* with a red Ferrari, while another with a black Lamborghini. And then you will have the odd car fancier who will tell you that the best sports car is a 1970s GTO. Likely not many of the others will know that what you had in mind when you said *sports car* was a silver 1961 Porsche. Let's take this idea little further into business communication.

Perhaps you have a colleague who has written a report and hands it to you for approval before it can be sent to a client. You may look at the report and find that the prose seems stilted, almost as if the writer really didn't want to be talking. Or you may find the writer tried to use every word that was mentioned on the SAT exam. So you may hand the report back to the writer and say, "Make it sound a little less formal." To you *informal* means adding more readability; to the person who wrote it, *informal* may mean it doesn't have to be perfect and he can write the way he talks outside of work. You may mean to get rid of the three-dollar words; he may take the remark to mean it's okay for him to use slang and street language. Maybe he assumes you meant to call the CEO of the client company by his first name. Or perhaps he's just not quite sure what you meant. All sorts of misunderstandings are possible.

Be specific. A chair is a chair. A 1961 Porsche is a 1961 Porsche. A bunch of daffodils from Trader Joe's is a bunch of daffodils from Trader Joe's. Leave no room for doubt and everyone is happy.

Be Active

In E.B. White's writing bible *Elements of Style,* one of the rules he gives for good writing is to eliminate all unnecessary passive voice.[1] (That's a grammatical term—but just because it is, you don't get to hide in your hoodie and pretend I didn't say anything.) Understanding passive voice and how to convert it to active voice is one of the quickest and easiest ways to increase clarity in your writing.

So what is passive voice? Think for a moment about a passive person. Does this person do anything—or are things done unto him? Things are done unto him. He just sits, waiting for someone else to do the action. Passive voice construction, whether in writing or speaking, behaves the same way. While good and clear communication inspires thought, action, analysis, and response, passive voice remains hidden in that hoodie, waiting for someone else to do the work. It is acted upon instead of acting.

How does one recognize passive voice? Through observation and focus. Look carefully at the sentence's construction in detail, starting with the verb. Why the verb? Because the verb is the action of the sentence, and

---

[1]Clarity is not about more. It is about enough.

therefore it conveys what one means. A good sentence always has a good verb; in fact, you could say that the sentence revolves around the verb. So to break down the sentence, first find the verb in the sentence that follows:

The ball was thrown by John.

Your immediate reaction is that the verb is *thrown.* But doing deeper observation and using focus, you will then see that the word *was* is also a verb—a helping verb. You may want to rush things and decide right now whether the verb is active or passive. But in good Zen manner, we need to contemplate all pieces before we rush into action.

So we now look for the subject that goes with the verb. Like a pair of socks, verbs and their subjects go together, and we need to look at them as a pair. Never mind the grammatical aspect here; use the easy test to find the verb's mate. Just ask.

Take the verb and ask *who* or *what* did the verb. Here we would ask, "Who or what was thrown?" The answer is your subject. Here the answer is *the ball.*

Now we ask ourselves, *is the subject doing the action?* Or here: *Is the ball throwing or being thrown?* It's being thrown. Therefore, it isn't doing an action; it is being acted upon. It's passive. So what's wrong with passive? Well, in this sentence, the idea is fairly clear, due to the *by John* phrase. But take a look at this next example of passive voice:

Salaries were reduced last week.

It's a passive sentence, but don't take my word for it: walk through the steps. What's the verb? *Reduced*—but you also have *were reduced.* Yep. The complete verb is *were reduced.* Who or what was reduced? *Salaries.* Seems clear.

But using your deep Zen observation skills, you'll see that while on the surface the sentence seems clear, it leaves several questions unanswered. Who reduced them? Why? For how long? By how much? When did it happen? We really don't know. And unless we ask those questions, we allow the communicator to weasel out of communicating a clear thought.

To fix that passive voice, we ask those questions. We probe and see the whole picture. And gradually clarity appears. Observe:

Last week, after the third disappointing sales quarter in a row, XYZ's management voted to reduce salaries for exempt employees by 5% for the next six months. XYZ hopes that it will be able to restore this cut once sales pick up.

See the difference? Make it active, and the whole picture appears.

Zen encourages us to take action only when we know what the action should be.

To know that, we have to see the whole picture.

Avoid Repetition

Another thing to think about when you're trying to achieve clarity is how often you repeat yourself. My friend Terri Hoover, who is a prize-winning mystery writer, has a rule that I love: if you have to write a second sentence to explain the one you just wrote, that means the first sentence stinks. In the Terry Hoover rule, you realize that your thoughts were not well focused in the first sentence, so you subconsciously fine tune and refocus the sentence for greater clarity.

To apply the Terry Hoover rule, use a simple technique: simply cut the first sentence. Usually you will find that your first sentence prose is not needed at all. If you do need any of it, normally all you will need is a word or two from the first sentence simply because your mind subconsciously reformatted and made the idea clear. Nothing can be simpler.

However, applying the Terri Hoover rule takes a great deal of willpower and a great deal of self-reflection. In Zen, we learn to let go of attachments that are not necessary. We learn to look at the world objectively, not subjectively, and to look at the world about us, not ourselves. But looking at our writing is sometimes hard to do.

How to avoid repetition? The best way is to print a copy, get out of your chair, and read it as if someone were listening. Actually reading it to someone is especially effective. (Dogs are great for this exercise. Cats don't care.) As you read, you will hear the repetition. You will hear your attempts at explaining your first sentence. You'll hear when you continue to harp on the same point. You will hear the words that are repeated—and repeated. Keep a pen or highlighter with you as you read. Mark the excess verbiage. Then go back to your document and cut away.

Keep It Short

Another test to help you with clarity is to ensure your sentences avoid carrying too much content in a jumble of ideas. Just as we took paragraphs and cut them down to no more than 12 tight lines in a printed document or six lines in an electronic document, we now need to look at sentence length.

How long should a good sentence be? If we use the third grade English teacher answer, we have to say at a minimum that sentences should have at least a subject and verb. That's all you really need: that subject and verb. So how do you judge then, when you add more, what's enough and what's too much?

Both Zen and yoga are very conscious of the breath, and writing with and consciousness is no different. Being aware of how much one can actually say without having to pause for air gives you a very good guideline for how much you should actually write in a sentence.

Again we go back to your body and how things work in nature. Most people cannot take in more information as they read and can say in one breath. When you read your work aloud, if you're running out of breath, then you have too much in the sentence. Use that knowledge. The easy way to fix the clarity is to hear where you've run out of breath: somewhere in the area you will have a conjunction, a comma, or transitional device. Break the sentence there and start a new sentence.

"Hey!" you're saying, "I thought the sentences of educated people contain big words and lots of ideas—the longer the better." This idea unfortunately is propagated by too far too many well-meaning high school English teachers who tell you that they want *more* in your writing. Where the disconnect occurs is that *more* does not always mean more words. It usually means more clarity or more depth; it could also mean adding examples and answers to the 5 W's to explain your idea. It could mean adding more tightness. But rarely does it mean to add more words.

To add to our confusion, most of us have received paper assignments that specified a certain number of words. Those instructions unfortunately again encourage us to add lots more verbiage. Why? For most of us, that "more" needs to be clarified. "More," in correct terms, means *tell me more about what you just said; you haven't given me enough detail to understand what you mean.* And again we have to understand that to answer that question, we don't need to add more words; we need to add more thought.

While this explanation sounds contradictory, consider the following example. How deeply do you think? Do you clutter your mind with all sorts of non-essentials, mentally changing channels as you thought surf? While surfing sometimes brings in great ideas and allows us to relax enough to let brilliance in, most of us accumulate clutter mentally. And then we add piles on top of piles of unclear statements, hoping like heck to somehow send the message that's necessary. Or we add data, believing that data is information. It isn't; data is just data. It needs to be interpreted and explained to have any meaning.

But do you think about that fact before you write? Do we just change mental channels, saying "Been there seen that" and moving on? If so, put down the mental remote. Stay put. Look around. What's going on in this scenario? Who all is involved? Who needs to be involved? What are the undercurrents? What is the social context?

Take time to simplify. Study details—but don't keep every minute detail. Pack lightly; take along only what is necessary. By eliminating what you don't need, you increase your clarity. You can't know what you will need until you do your deep thinking. How does each item connect to the next? Have you made that clear? Or is your connection still only in your head? Have you hidden it? Have you assumed anything? Have you said the same thing several times, only in a slightly different manner? Simplify. Keep only what you need.

CHAPTER 8

Embrace the Fear

You must never feel badly about making mistakes... as long as you take the trouble to learn from them. For you often learn more by being wrong for the right reasons than you do by being right for the wrong reasons.

— Norton Juster, *The Phantom Tollbooth*

About this time you may be saying to yourself, "I don't know about all of this. You keep saying it's simple. But it sounds hard. I'm afraid I won't remember all of this." Hear that big whooshing sound in the background? That's fear—the big energy suck of modern life.

One thing many people don't like to admit is that often they are afraid. We're afraid we can't get our work done if we stop to read someone else's poorly written prose. We're afraid we will miss something and look stupid so we write a bunch of gobbledegook, hoping no one will notice. And once in a while, as we are sitting in front of the computer, hurriedly zapping out the emails as fast as we can so we can get back to our own work, a situation comes about where we are literally afraid to answer.

These challenging situations can include answering an angry vendor or an overly aggressive colleague who has sent a terse and almost offensive email, or composing a reply or follow-up to your boss. Perhaps we aren't really sure what the boss has asked us, when the deadline for the project is due, or what all needs to be in the completed project. We then really don't know how to say, "I didn't understand what you wanted me to do." Never mind that the responsibility of making the instructions clear lies with the boss; we still have to deal with it. And often we sit there, afraid to say anything.

Fear steals our emotional time. By making us react to the emotions that the situation brings, not to the situation itself, we negate or slow down any needed action. Think about how much time we spend dreading something. Now try to quantify it. Reluctant to face the email or conversation with the employee whose tone or inability to get her work done on time is slowing down your own productivity? How many times does the thought "I need to do something about this" cross your mind—and then how many times do you have to deal with the sinking feeling in your stomach when you think about handing it?

Fear steals our physical time. We put off sending the message, so it stays there in our mental inbox. And like any formidable mass, it grows. It keeps blocking the forward motion of our other tasks, merely by existing. It continues to be there, taking up time we could be using elsewhere. Try quantifying the time you spend on putting off dealing with just this sort of message: if it crosses your mind at least three times a day, and if the thought takes 30 seconds, that's a minute and a half.

But wait! There's more. The thought doesn't come as a stand-alone product; it also has that fear attached to it. The fearful emotional reaction takes at least twice as long—the 30 seconds that the fear reacts in your body, and then at least another minute to have your rational brain counter with "I can't think about that now; I have other work to do." But then you also experience lag speed in your next few minutes as your body tries to normalize itself from that momentary flight-or-fight action. So let's say that you lose six minutes at the minimum—and that's probably low as most of us take longer, either to recover from the reaction or in the number of times we think about dreaded task. And let's say you put it off for six days. That means the fear has stolen *at a minimum* a half hour of your precious time, as well as your balance and well-being.

Let's break down why you may be afraid of writing.

Fear of Revision

Many people feel that once they have written something, they're done. It is therefore written in stone. Or they hate the idea of being judged for their writing. Or they hate the idea of having to think deeply in order to have something to say. In any of these cases, the result is the same: they put down each word as if it is another inch in the crawl to cross a desert. This goal isn't to do it well. The goal is to get it done. This belief leads to several problems.

One, many people are afraid to write. They are afraid that they will be judged by what is put down on that piece of paper. And they are usually partially right: many people do judge you by your written words. But that does not mean that the very first set of words that you write is what has to stand as the final version. It simply means that writing, like almost anything else, is not a piece of your soul; it's a piece of your work. Your soul is not judged by a one-time action, but by an accumulation of actions. It's judged by many incarnations, many revisions, and many chances to atone for mistakes.

In Zen Buddhism, life is all about revision and making things better.

Writing is no different. You write down the first words, and they will probably stink. But you don't stop there. Stopping and thinking, "I've put down the words and I'm now done" is the quickest way to defeat progress. The secret to progressing in writing, just as it is in Zen, is that each time you revise, you create a new wrinkle in your brain that takes the initial action that occurs the next time to a slightly higher level than it was in the first action. So if you write something, and then take the time to revise it mindfully, your brain learns to write in the revised, more mindful manner—and will use that manner for the initial writing the next time you sit down to write. That means that each successive revision leads to a higher level of writing for the rest of your writing life. That's very powerful stuff.

Theologian and writer Anne Lamott emphasizes this point in her book *Bird by Bird*[1] when she explains that her writer father taught her brother to write when the young boy was assigned a large project on birds. When the boy asked how to go about meeting this huge assignment, Lamott's father said he had to do it in steps: bird by bird. And each successive bird became easier to write about.

Writing isn't etching in stone. It is fluid, changing, growing—much like life. The people who are afraid of revising—or too lazy to do so— do not see the bigger picture. Some people are afraid to let things go. They fear that they will fail somehow if they do, so they look for perfection as an ideal. These are the students who always ask for an extension because "I can make it better" or the people who never stop fiddling with their Powerpoint slides.

---

[1]Lamott, Anne (1994). *Bird by Bird.* New York, NY: Panthenon.

Zen teaches us that perfection is impossible; we are all works in process.

To have the self-compassion to accept that process, and to accept that our writing will be flawed in some way, but hey, it's the best I can do right now with the tools and skills I have, is a mighty act. We accept imperfection as growth and effort in others; accepting it in ourselves shows compassion and mercy and kindness. In other words, it embodies the principles of Zen.

But those who are afraid to see themselves as works in progress make life miserable for themselves. They set up a standard they will always fail to achieve. Really? Why do that to yourself? Everything has a time limit; everything has a cycle.

Another lesson from Zen is that one has to know when it's time to let go.

You have to know when it's time to move on. Sometimes people try to freeze their lives in routine or continuous repetition, running from the past but afraid of the future. They apply that constraint to their writing, afraid the final product won't be good enough. Here's the irony: nothing stays the same. It either progresses or regresses—even stagnation is regression. So in that endless revision, they are actually regressing—by taking themselves right back to where they started.

Remember the movie *Groundhog Day*? Bill Murray's character is caught in over a hundred endless replays of the same day. Sometimes he makes the same mistake he made in previous versions. Sometimes he does something different with a different result. Along the way, he learns to play the piano and speak another language and becomes a much different person from the first time he experienced the day—but he keeps waking up in the morning, caught in the same day, until he realizes that he has changed and is ready to move on.

People who cannot stop themselves from rewriting and trying to make something perfect need to realize one simple truth: they alone are the ones who can move things along. Only by letting go of that fear of being less than perfect can their writing—and their lives—grow. And by doing so, they show that compassion for themselves. One way to reach that point is to ask, "How important is it? Is this particular piece of writing worth this much time?" A technique that helps it to figure out exactly how much money you make on average per hour. Then break that down into how much you earn per minute. Let's say, for instance, that you make $30 an hour. Basically you make $.50 per minute. If that one email sentence you're working on takes you up to 10 minutes to compose, then that one sentence alone costs you five dollars. And that's just one sentence—not the whole email!

If the email has three sentences, and you have put $5 into each, you have to ask yourself if the end result of that email is worth those $15. Some are, but most aren't. Only you can answer that question. In your preparation time and thoughts before you write, set a limit for what you are willing to spend on the piece of. You may not want to work on this one sentence more than three minutes; you may not want to work on the whole email more than three minutes. So before you start, you set a time budget. The time budget limit allows you to decide on the level of clarity you can achieve in the limited time, given the tools and skills and circumstances you have right now. You will have learned something from it; the next time you will move higher, just because you were aware as you composed and revised.

Whether you are a one-and-done or a constant tinkerer, you still have to get distance from your writing. As we said earlier, it is a piece of your work, not a piece of your soul. Allowing yourself that objectivity will allow you to revise and cut, which in turn will lend itself to much easier reading and much clearer communication.

Fear of Reaction

Why are we afraid? Because we don't want to face someone else's reaction. We are afraid of conflict. Conflict is going to exist. Avoiding the issue, or being afraid to confront the issue, doesn't make the conflict go away. As someone once put it, fear does not mean you forget everything and run; it means you face everything and rebound. Facing up to one's fears, choosing your words wisely, and going forward not only gives the image of great professionalism but also furthers communication. Without communication, the conflict can never be resolved.

And really, how much of a major impact is someone else's reaction going to have on you? In most cases, the reaction may be unpleasant, but it's not life-threatening. It's not like the situation that women in Sub-Sahara Sudan face, where facing any conflict may mean literally life or death. In the bigger picture, what it usually means that you have to look at yourself and what you need to do to grow or improve. In other words, even if the result of facing the conflict is positive, we still have to change. And as Woodrow Wilson reportedly once said, "If you want to make instant enemies, tell them they have to change."

As creatures of habit, we don't like change and growth, no matter how many times we say that we want it and even change jobs to "grow."

Taking a bigger view of any situation helps reduce fear. So you have an angry vendor. And you're dreading in some way answering him. Explore a bit: why? Just because you don't like conflict? That bigger picture makes you look at the details—not the details of what he is angry about, although those do matter, but what is causing your fear. What's he going to do, reach across the WiFi and choke you? Even if his words make you feel as if he is, in reality, that isn't going to happen. This fearful reaction is more about your emotional self overreacting than it is about your rational observation of what has caused the conflict in the first place. Focusing less on yourself and how you feel about the words and more about what the words indicate will not only reduce your fear but help solve the problem.

First, take a deep breath. This most likely isn't about you; it's most likely about an action that somehow has an attachment to you. It's about something you, or someone you are responsible for, did, not about what you are. Seen in perspective, this distinction should resolve fear. It may instead raise feelings of responsibility and ownership—and those don't involve fear. Using logic to see the details can help solve the conflict. So how do you put things in perspective?

Behavioral psychologists have an interesting technique to help patients who have panic attacks that are based on fear. This technique requires the patient to go into the fear and, instead of trying to bury it—and leaving it there to continue to grow and steal your time and energy—truly embrace the fear. That means imagining the worst. It means investing some time in imagining what could happen. So let's say you need to tell your boss that you didn't complete the project she assigned, mainly because you weren't sure what she wanted. You may know in your heart that her communication was vague and shoddy, but you are afraid that if you tell her you didn't understand—well, what *are* you afraid of?

Let's imagine it:

You: I have to tell you something. I know you wanted the Barker report finished and on your desk tomorrow.

Boss: That's right, and it had better be there. *(menacing look)*

You: It may not be.

Boss: What?! You fool! You imbecile! I need that report and I need it now! What's wrong with you? Why didn't you get it done? Too busy checking Facebook?

You: No, no—I, well, I—I didn't understand what you wanted me to do with it.

Boss: What do you mean you didn't understand what I wanted you to do it? My communication and email was perfectly clear. You are stupid. What is wrong with you? When I tell you to do something, of course my communication is perfect. I am going to write you up.

You: Please please no. Anything but that. My family and I need this job!

Now let's look at the bigger picture. Is this really going to happen? Unless you have the boss from hell, probably not. Look at the different opportunities you have to confront this fear and make this a positive conflict. Consider the point when the boss says "My communication is perfectly clear,"—I sincerely doubt that the boss will say those exact words. The unreasonable boss will say something such as, "What's not clear?" The reasonable boss will say something to you such as, "What part did you not understand?" Either way, the action you need to take now is the same. You can turn that whole scenario, with either boss, into a win for you both by sticking to the 5 W's and the WIFM. Observe:

You: I wasn't quite clear when you said that I needed to provide examples and to revise to make it more reader oriented, I didn't know whether you wanted me to actually give facts and figures, or to give examples and analogies that illustrate those figures. I understood the who, what, and the when, but I wasn't sure quite exactly where I needed to find the information. Also, if I know why exactly you wanted me to change these things, and your vision of how those changes would change my report and help me focus it to present us in the best possible light, I can give you exactly what you're looking for.

Boss   *(somewhat mollified):* Well that makes sense. Of course I thought you would know exactly how to do this section.

You: I have an idea, but I wanted to make sure that we were exactly on the same page. I don't want to waste your time *(to yourself: or mine.)*

Boss: Then why didn't you come to me when you first got the email?

You: Because I had a few earlier deadlines and just gave your email a quick for-now read and mistakenly thought that revisions wouldn't be as major as they are. I know I was wrong here, but I wasn't aware of just how bad the original report was until I had the time to read your notes carefully.

See?

The situation has diffused. You're now actually dealing with the situation and the actions associated with it, not with the emotions. And really, when you look at this in this bigger imaginary picture, you see the problems. Why didn't you go to the boss when you first got the email? Simply because you were afraid. Yes, you probably did have other earlier deadlines. But the quick for-now read? Somewhere in the back of your mind, you may have not wanted to face looking at the detailed feedback then.

But putting it off didn't make the situation any better. Had you gone with the boss first sent you the email, a week ago, not only would you have saved an awful lot of your own time, but hers too. Also, you would have come across as more confident, more professional, and more proactive.

You could have invested this half hour in knowing exactly what the boss wanted and learning for next time. And that investment would also be a great thing for your emotional well-being—unlike living in fear.

Seeing the bigger picture allows you to see your own responsibility. Sometimes allowing yourself to imagine the absolute worst will help you gain perspective. What if you imagined your boss getting mad and picking up a book end and throwing it at you—or stomping over and trying to choke you? Imagine it: She'd be hunched over your body, arms akimbo, snarling and trying to avoid your flailing hands while your eyes roll and your body shakes and your tongue lolls out like some character on Looney Toons.

That most likely is not going to happen. Yet pushing that really absurd and horrible possible reaction scenario reveals a lot about what we really fear. Most likely what we really fear is not going to happen, but imagining it will probably get it to the point where it's funny. Seeing the bigger picture allows you to lose the fear. It reveals the holes in your thinking. It shows you where you can create a better product. And it shows you how you yourself can grow and change.

Fear of Being Wrong or Less than Perfect

Many of us are also afraid of being wrong. Being wrong about something means that somehow *we* are wrong: not just this one opinion but ourselves as a whole. So we play it safe. I have seen students so worried about getting punctuation wrong that they write safe little See Jane Run sentences. They get the punctuation right, yes, mainly because they write sentences that require nothing but a final period, yet they lose depth of content. They lose ideas and creativity and spark. These Look! Look! Spot! There's nothing there! sentences actually send a message that something in us *is* wrong if we can't loosen up a bit to try.

Many of us don't have the self-confidence to feel as if we are good enough. We may be accepted to grad school, but spend the first few weeks in class thinking, "They made a mistake. I'm too stupid to be here. I don't know any of this stuff." (Some poor souls spend their entire grad school career thinking this way.) Well, of course you don't know any of this stuff: you came to grad school to learn it. If you knew it all, what would be the point?

Or maybe we are afraid that if we are wrong on one little tiny thing, the rest of the world will think we are imposters, not worthy of perhaps even life itself. Balderdash! Life is about growing.

> Zen teaches us that learning and making progress—not perfection—on the way is the purpose of life.

Yet the statement is not embraced well in modern-day Western thought. We pay lip service to learning by mistakes but punish if any mistakes occur. We fear being judged so harshly that we prevent and protect our kids from ever making mistakes. Think about the parent who does the science project, so the kid will get a good grade (and yes, I bet you know at least three of them). The problem becomes, however, that by doing so we send a message that the kids by themselves are not good enough to do the task. Or that they aren't strong enough.

We fail to see the bigger picture once again. And we teach that the outcome is more important than the effort. Remember that old saw about Thomas Edison making a thousand mistakes before he invented the light bulb? You didn't see his parents hanging around trying to do it for him. And as a result, he wasn't afraid to be wrong. He knew who he was, and he was confident that he would be able to make his invention work, even if it took him a thousand tries.

Alina Tugend, in her book *Better by Mistake: The Unexpected Benefits of Being Wrong* (2011), offers evidence that making mistakes is so important that even people who have been recognized as saints have made them:

As Thomas Caughwell, author of the pithily named book Saints Behaving Badly, *put it: 'The Catholic calendar is full of notorious men and women who turned their lives around and become saints. St. Camillus de Lellis was an Italian mercenary soldier, a card sharp and con man. For six years St. Margaret of Cortona lived as a Tuscan nobleman's mistress. St. Moses the Egyptian led a gang of cutthroats in the Egyptian dessert. And St. Pelagia was the porn queen of fifth-century Antioch.' Of course, they went through great suffering to become saints—but the point is, they made their fair share of mistakes. And most of us aren't aiming for canonization. (p. 37)*

Makes you think twice about avoiding that conversation with your boss, doesn't it?

Compassion Is the Key to Overcoming Fear

Right about now many of you are thinking, "Why should I have to do these things? These people I interact with are adults. They should know how to write professionally!" Yes. They should. But that doesn't mean that they do. Many of them have never been taught, some of them don't understand what they were taught, and others have forgotten what they were taught. Instead of thinking, "Oh my heavens, why can't this jerk get his life together?" approach it from a Zen perspective.

That perspective espouses that we need to care for all living things. It's called having compassion. Even the lowliest ant or bug is too precious to be squashed in the Zen point of view. This idea is in line with the Golden Rule that some of us grew up with.

No matter what you call it, if we treat others the way we would like to be treated ourselves, we find that our vision opens deeply.

What does that mean? It means that by opening vision, we see clearly. We suddenly see the audience in its entirety—and we also see beyond our own perspectives. By doing so, we increase the clarity and sharpness of what we are asking of others, which in turn increases, focuses, and sharpens our instructions and our words. To do so, you have to think about this whole task in a compassionate way. Instead of thinking *this guy should know how to write professionally*, we have to look at what he is doing in a positive manner. Therefore, the positive spin on this thought is *he's trying hard to be professional. I have to give him credit for that; he really wants to do a good job. It's up to me to show compassion and teach him how to take one more step up on his own path toward professionalism.*

Think about yourself in a compassionate way as well. Most of us talk to ourselves in a manner in which we would never talk to anyone else. Do you berate yourself for making small mistakes? For being less than perfect? Toward the end of his life, the great 20th century poet W.H. Auden tried repeatedly but unsuccessfully to erase the poetry that had made him famous, saying it was no longer honest and truly wasn't good enough. Yet it was good enough for Auden to have been lauded as one of the best poets of his generation; his poetry is still read and studied by hundreds of thousands of high school and college students every year.

How much more compassionate it would have been for Auden to have accepted his younger self and that younger self's work. It was honest at the time he wrote it. But as his skills developed and his poetry became more perfected, he failed to accept the reality of growth.

> We are all creatures on the path to enlightenment, so we should celebrate that we took that step, that we tried. If we have made even a miniscule of progress, we've grown.

Moreover, what's hard for some of us isn't hard for others—and sometimes what is easy for some is hard for others. We don't always see that truth. We just judge ourselves by abstract ideas of perfectionism instead of evaluating each step toward excellence. Let's face it; sometimes it's okay to do a B-level job, if that's all you can do in the circumstances you have going on in your life. Sometimes it's a victory just to have done something at all.

Have a little compassion. Pat yourself on the back, smile, and get back on the horse. Fear is false expectations appearing real (or forgetting everything and running). Compassion is embracing the passion, the life force that flows through all of us. As the old saw goes, we are all humans being, doing the best we can. Remember that.

By doing so, both you and the person who was trying to be as professional as possible take another step on the path to enlightenment. By having compassion for him and seeing the positives of what he is doing, you clarify your instructions and smooth out your tongue. You build a win-win. And you both progress.

CHAPTER 9

Honor the Reader

We ought to be vigilantes for kindness and consideration.

—Letitia Baldrige

Once you have grasped the "it's not about me" concept of good business writing, and have paid attention to the audience, structure, and details before you start to write, you're ready to move beyond the basics.

The medium you use for sending can increase the effectiveness of your message. Framing your message in a positive manner can increase the chances that your audience will be more receptive to your message. Using the right tone can help ensure the success of your message. And thinking before you hit Send can save your professional career.

Respect the Medium

Imagine this situation: You're sitting in a meeting and suddenly your boss starts referring to an email he sent the week before; you and the rest of the attendees are apparently supposed to not only know which email he is referring to but know the questions he asked in the email. You receive over 70 emails per day—on a light day—so this particular email would have been almost 500 emails ago (like most Americans, you're supposed to check your work email on weekends). Try as you might, you can't remember the email, much less the questions.

Moreover, your boss has a tendency to send lots of background emails, and you're not always sure how the content applies to you. He also tends to ask rhetorical questions, so you aren't sure when you are supposed to have an answer or when you are just supposed to see your boss's thinking on the subject.

And so you sit, uncomfortable, feeling like a kid in the third grade who's hoping the teacher won't call on him, worried that by missing that one email you have sabotaged your career. The reality is that, even though your boss may rage and fume at you, this situation is most likely not your fault. In this time of technology so many of us—and especially those who hold positions of power and who have to juggle many responsibilities— feel that because we sent the message, we have communicated.

As we've noted, communication doesn't take place until the receiver understands not only the message, but also the words and the context of the message. Communication doesn't take place until she understands the emotions and the importance of it, as well as what he is supposed to do with the contents of the message. Only when those complex processes take place does communication take place.

Technology is a beautiful thing in many ways. But just because sending messages via email is easy for a manager to do doesn't mean it is the right way to communicate the ideas.

Consider this true story:

On a particular day in May 2001, at 10:00 a.m., IT employees in the benefits department of a large nationally traded company found that their desktop computers suddenly locked. After the employees spent 15 minutes trying to troubleshoot the problem, the computers unlocked themselves, whereupon a banner began scrolling across all the screens. It read:

> *Your department has been outsourced and sold. This is your 90-day notice; individual compensation packages will be discussed in 30 days, when we have had a chance to evaluate you individually. However, you are prohibited from seeking another job during this 90-day period; otherwise the compensation package will be revoked.*

Not a good way to announce layoffs. The sister of one of these employees happened to be a very high-powered lawyer, who was more than happy to write a letter that stated intent to investigate the legal damages the employees could receive from this manner of message delivery. Through her investigation, she learned that the department had been sold to a small start-up, whose two owners, while very skilled in IT and in benefits, were astonished that their medium for their message was inappropriate. They truly believed that because it was easy for them to send the message that way, it was the right way.

The lawyer sister filed a class action suit, claiming that delivering emotionally charged messages via business email is unprofessional and a form of harassment. She won. The employees all received not only large outsourcing packages, but even larger damages.

Email, instant messages, and texts are good for rapid delivery of messages. They do not, however, allow the sender to see the first impact of the message on the receiver. For this reason, impersonal technology channels aren't typically the best medium for sending messages that affect people's livelihoods.

The phone call medium is also tricky. In the old days, your business phone was tied to a cord that was attached in the wall in an area of a specific building that was your place of employment. You left it at 5 p.m. on Fridays and didn't have to worry about it until Monday. And during the week, if you were out of the office, someone would answer your phone and handle the caller's needs or take a message for you, written on a nice pink piece of paper.

But phones today are different. One executive I know carries three cell phones daily—and none of them are her personal cell phone. One is for her direct reports to use, one is for the top administration to use to reach her quickly, and one is for emergency contact in case she is using one of the other phones. With that number of devices for her work associates to reach her, no wonder she was irritated one Sunday when she was at church—and a colleague called her about work on her personal cell phone.

A call on a business line has a less personal touch than does a call on a personal line. Yet while the issue may not emotionally impact the receiver, your use of his personal line may send an unintended message that you aren't respecting that person's personal space.

Despite all the talk in business today about work-life balance, technology can blur the lines and make that balance impossible.

Using the correct medium helps keep that balance. Many productivity experts recommend that we designate only certain times a day to check email. Others recommend all sorts of systems to have email sort itself automatically. The aim is to be able to actually get your work done. So if you choose email as your medium and need an instant response, chances are good you won't get it instantaneously. Do you need a quick one-sentence answer? Try a text or instant message. Need a quick but longer answer? Text first to see if it's a good time for a quick phone call.

> To honor the medium successfully you have to know your audience well, and you have to know your goals. You also have to do a lot of strategic thinking about how best to send the message.

Are these hard and fast rules? No. The reason that honoring the medium is a beyond-basics skill is that no real rules exist. Guidelines, however, do.

Is your audience made up mainly of *visual learners?* In other words, do they use phrases such as *I see what you mean* or *look at what opportunities we have here?* These people usually like to read, as long as the document is organized. They like graphs, but only if they say something and are simple. For these types, create a verbal picture in your message and you're gold. They don't like to be talked at, and they can read faster than you can talk, so don't expect a good response when you read from your Prezi or PowerPoint.

And what if your audience is highly visual but also highly *energetic?* Don't email them a PowerPoint via email that contains data that you could put in a quick bullet list or in one visual. These folks usually chafe during webinars that don't move quickly. They see so much more on their screens than the main presentation box and want to move on, and move on now.

On the other hand, *audial learners*, those who use phrases such as *listen to what the data is telling us* or *hear me"* like those Powerpoints. They like the webinars; those allow them to focus on how the information is said. These people usually process more slowly than the visuals—but often they wind up picking up more details. So if your boss or client is visual and busy, put the majority of your time into a document that lets him see at one glance not only what your points are but also give him an interesting and unusual visual cue to keep in his mind. But if he's audial, polish your words and practice your delivery. Then make sure you get one-on-one time to deliver your ideas verbally.

Tactile learners like to experience what you are talking about. Craft your message so that you put them in what the English professors call *in medias res*, or in the middle of the action. (That's how the opening of this section was worded; it was intended to make you feel as if you were in the situation.)

And *intuitive* types are usually following their own thought patterns, no matter how structured your message. Be prepared for lots of unexpected stops in thought with these folks, and have patience with what may appear as off-topic ideas. Many *non-intuitives* lack that patience with intuitives, unaware that those detours often reveal the brilliance and creativity that all successful businesses need.

Remain focused on the fact that you are marketing your ideas to your audience. And doing some deep thinking about how best to market and by what medium increases your professionalism as well as success.

Framing Your Ideas

Ever heard the phrase *frame of mind?*

A *frame* is a negotiations term that means to place information in a way that the other party—in this case, the audience—can most easily understand.

When we use an analogy, for instance, we are putting something in a frame. Saying that a conversation should be like playing a game of ping pong frames the image of two players, each perfectly matched, sending verbal balls back and forth to each other. That's a frame.

But one big problem exists in using frames: very few of us have the same frame. Place six people at an event and have them watch, all from the same physical perspective. Then ask them what they saw. You will get six different versions of what happened, simply because each person saw the event differently.

We are all products of our environment. Those environments include subtle social and relationship cues that affect how we perceive what we are hearing or seeing. How we perceive what we are reading or hearing is also influenced by our moods at the time, our history with the material, our history with the sender of the message, comprehension of the message, and the role we are playing at the time of receiving the message.

Sounds like a lot? It *is* a lot, and for us to sort through all of those things in the instant we take in the message, we have to sort through all the complexities that each message carries with it. To do so, we rely on a series of shortcuts, which are reactions that come from what Malcolm

Gladwell refers to as "the locked box" of our subconscious. Our shortcuts, however, are notoriously faulty. And they lead to many perceptual distortions, which in turn lead to many otherwise perfectly crafted messages to fall short of communicating. Being aware of these perceptual distortions can help you frame your message so that you're heard.

Let's take stereotyping, which is one of the most common perceptual distortions, and look at how being aware of it can help you communicate. Imagine that you are the head of the IT department for a large firm. You're a well-rounded multi-faceted business professional and know your business well. But every time you send out an email, your message carries with it the stereotypical image of an IT worker: brainy, nerdy, socially clueless—and most likely a man.

In fact, people see your name in the sender's line, and unless they have lots of personal experience with you, think, "Oh, IT message. Details I won't understand" or other variations along the same lines. You may have worked hard to get your headline up front and to be short and reader-centered, but that message still has to break through the knee-jerk stereotype reaction. Knowing that tendency to stereotype, the frame you use to craft your message is vital. While those in the accounting or HR departments might get away with subject lines that read "important year-end information" (although I doubt it), you certainly can't. People may read that line and think, "I don't need anything at year end from IT' and delete your message before it's even been opened.

So think about the frame. Despite the incredibly hard work that IT folks do to make sure that the rest of us have effective technology in our jobs, we tend to dismiss or forget that hard work. Instead, we see only our own use of technology, and increasingly we see using that technology as our right. We see it as a tool to serve us. And the IT people are only there to see that it does.

You and I both know that is faulty perception. It's perceptual distortion. But if you're smart and want your message read, you acknowledge that like it or not, that's how many see messages from IT, and you then plot to frame your message accordingly. Therefore, wording your subject line "Helpful Tech Tool Tips to make your year-end less crazy" frames your "year-end information" in a frame that other people will likely see as vital. And despite the stereotype, they read your message.

Two other common perceptual distortions are *selective perception* and *projection*.

> Selective perception occurs when the reader singles out information in the message that confirms a prior belief but ignores any information that is contrary to his opinion or to what he wants to hear.

Being aware of that distortion that results from selective perception can help you frame the message so that even if the receiver doesn't agree with your conclusion, you can at least stop the back-and-forth "because I said so," and "I said so in the past three emails" dance.

Imagine, for instance, that you have an employee who really wants the company to pay for her to attend a conference coming up next month. You as boss don't have the money in the budget that it will cost to send her. If you write back,

Ashley, we don't have the money in the budget for you to attend.

She may come back at you with

Meredith is going, and the information I will learn at the conference applies more to my job than it does to hers.

See what is going on in this reply? She ignored the contrary part, which is that the budget can't send her. Instead she went right to singling out the information that confirms her prior belief: the material applies to her so she should go, not Meredith. Never mind that she has reverted to the level of 10-year-old whining because her sister got something and she didn't. That's her frame of mind, and without your being aware of it, you are primed for a very long and upsetting disagreement about the issue.

However, by framing your message so that you send the message to Ashley that you are aware that the material applies to her job, and while you would like to be able to send both employees, the present budget won't allow it, you stop the disagreement. This wording might work better:

Ashley, the conference does indeed seem as if it would help your job. I wish you had put in a request to go back when Meredith did, before

the budget for the quarter was finalized; that way I could possibly have sent you both. Keep an eye on the conference for next year and make sure that you get your request in at least three months in advance; I look forward to all that you will learn at it next year!

Such wording confirms her prior belief, that she can benefit from it, and then talks her down from resistance so she can see how she can attend, albeit next year.

Projection occurs when we take what we are feeling a certain way about an issue and automatically assume that the other person feels that way too. If the receiver is feeling negative about the message, he may automatically believe, by projection, that you feel negatively, too. Ever gotten an email and thought, "*how dare she?*" and automatically become angry? That's projection. Ever sent a message, assuming the answer will be *yes*, because you want it to be so much? That's projection. Ever write a message afraid of what the possible outcomes could be? That's projection.

> The best way to overcome projection as a writer is to follow the Zen belief of keeping your head where your feet are.

Many of us have our feet in today but our heads in tomorrow; this adage implies, in other words, for us to stop that and stay right in the moment. Stay focused, instead of quickly thinking, *I just can't wait until I hear back from Beverly about my idea! It's such a good one!* Stay in the moment. Really examine all the sides and aspects of your idea and make sure you delineate all the aspects of it. Doing so keeps you in the present, and it destroys projection.

Also be aware of what the receiver could be projecting on you. Acknowledging that the projection is going on will help prevent any misunderstanding. If Beverly writes back: *This just isn't feasible at this time*, you're going to be very disappointed—and most likely angry as well. The anger arises because you have projected a certain future, and that future ideal isn't a reality. So your emotions get in the game.

However, Beverly can frame her response to deal successfully with the projection:

Wow! Sounds as if you are really excited about this idea. And it does have many great points to it. Unfortunately, some things are going on in the business that you most likely are unaware of right now, and those things will keep us from putting this idea in place right now. However, I would love to hear more about your idea so that we can keep it in mind for the future; when's a good time for us to do coffee?

Another way Beverly can frame the idea is by emphasizing outcomes or goals rather than the certain issue at hand. Beverly could have asked you how the idea fit in with the stated yearly departmental goals; if it didn't, you would discover that in the process of answering her. Some other common frames are people's aspirations and sense of identities; understanding those and framing your message to work nicely with those frames is more likely to get you a desired response.

Often business people use sports or military analogies or wording to frame their messages, hoping to make the message visual. Before the 1980s or so, this use of sports and military metaphors often discriminated against many women in business. In today's post-Title IX world, however, women aren't the ones who may not identify with the frame. Being aware of the globally diverse composition of today's workforce can keep you from framing your message in American baseball terms (a *grand slam*, for instance) that soccer-loving Europeans may have trouble translating.

In conclusion, understanding and using frames is really all about respecting your reader.

Respect the Font

So does the font matter?

Well, look at the issue this way. You may think that a fun font such as Bradley Hand or Comic Sans sets your message apart and identifies you as someone other than commonplace. However, to busy people who are scrolling and trying to read over 30 emails an hour, using these fonts can backfire on you. You could come across as self-centered or just plain old difficult to deal with.

Many of us use Times New Roman, simply out of habit, since universities and citation governing bodies such as APA and MLA require that our work be in that font. According to a Bloomberg study, however, the best fonts to use to send your message are Georgia and Verdana. Georgia ensures that the last stroke of the letter is darker and therefore more readable, while Verdana has better spacing. Verdana is also preferable for meeting accessibility standards because it is easier to read.

Bloomberg's study also advises against using Arial and Helvetica. The letters in Arial are too similar; the b and the d are exactly the same character, only reversed. And to someone scanning quickly, these characters can become confusing. Helvetica is cramped and just plain old hard to read.

Respect the Send Button

Ever got one of those "someone wishes to recall the last message" emails?

If you have, and you are like most people, instead of saying, "Yes, So-and-So does not want me to read that email" and deleting it, you read that email anyway just to see what that person did not want you to read. And then you begin to wonder why the person wanted to recall it.

People frequently fall victim to the trigger-happy send syndrome. They are so intent on getting the message off their plates that they fail to consider whether the message says what they meant. Throughout this book we have considered the importance of about taking your time. Being in the moment allows you to produce quality work, which in turn saves you time.

> Because a Zen approach involves acting deliberately, not chaotically, it means that you think before you act.

Being in the moment means thinking with 100 percent of your concentration on the task at hand, not completing it while you're thinking about what you're going to do next or what you will have for dinner when you get home from work. But we have already discussed taking your time. The question is How?

Several techniques exist to help you avoid the trigger-happy send syndrome. You can use any number of apps that will temporarily shut down your access to the Internet; if you use Gmail or Outlook, these will prohibit you from being able to send the email. You can even set up Outlook to delay delivery of messages. But you still have to go back and proofread what you wrote.

Another simple but very helpful technique is to make good use of your drafts box. While you may be in a hurry to get the email off and to get on with the rest of your life, and while you may have every good intention of focusing in a Zen-like manner on the message in front of you, human nature usually takes control of the steering mechanism. It drives you forward, taking you away from your sense of clarity and moves you quietly into thinking about the next task. That's where the drafts box becomes helpful. You use your best Zen-like approach to writing your email. But before you hit Send, first look a little further left on your options menu. Instead of sending the email, move it into your drafts box.

Then proceed to put 100 percent of your concentration on the next email. Focus on it, use the WIFM and the 5 W's approach, with your headline upfront, and write. But don't hit Send on this one either; move it into the drafts box. Once you're in the drafts box, go back to the first email that you moved there. Read it. Chances are very good you will find something to change, add, or tweak; very few things are ever perfect in the first incarnation. Fix those errors, add the extra information or cut the unnecessary junk. Doing so should take you no more than 60 seconds. But by reviewing before you hit Send, you have a better message and a clearer document. Only when you have given the email this drafts-box cool-and-correct editing minute do you then hit Send.

Why does this technique work? Because when we write, we are so intent on living in the middle of our own thoughts and messages that the self gets in the way. That sense of ego, that sense of self, often keeps us from doing our most effective work. By moving into another message and putting all of your concentration into that new message and into another topic, you move out of the self-absorption of the first message.

As a result, when you go back to read the second message, you see it in its entirety, not as a message in creation. You see it as the reader would see it. You don't see it as a product of your mind; you see it as a separate being from your own identity and self. Therefore, you can see things to fix, even if all you do is put your cursor at the end of one line, enter, and separate a long block of prose.

You may be saying at this point "But I don't have that kind of time!" Ironically, you don't have the kind of time *not* to do this. Moving that email into the drafts box takes the same amount of time is hitting Send; going back and rereading it takes less than a minute. You may be investing less than 60 seconds at the most. Yet by investing 60 seconds, you add to the value of your email by adding clarity, conciseness, and readability. That in turn makes your readers feel more favorable when they receive your message; they are aware on some level that you have done your best to help them understand the message, which often means you have helped them do their work in an easier and more efficient manner.

By this simple investment of a matter of seconds, you have strengthened the relationship between you and your reader, and you have moved it into a positive zone. You have invested in creating a network, a team, or a partnership. You gain allies, not frustrated readers who wonder where in the world you got your degree, and why you are still employed by the company. Instead of staking out a small self-absorbed zone of your own little world, you connect; you become one with your greater organization and your greater consciousness. If that is not the definition of an effective team player, I do not know what it is.

You also gain time by not having to recall messages, answer follow-up emails, or clear up details. You will be surprised to know what investing those few seconds can do for your writing and your professional image. Just avoid trying to hit that send button as quickly as possible.

A Non-Zen Observation

Zen operates in the realm of what is and that we should accept it.

Honoring the reader does indeed accept the reality of the reader and meets him on his own terms. However, understanding how to use the medium, the frames, and the delayed send button benefits us as the writer as well. As the infamous (and definitely not Zen) writer Machiavelli noted, the end justifies the means. And if the end is a message that is received and a work environment where people feel respected and heard, I'd say the means were justified.

CHAPTER 10

Honor the Positive

Our focus determines our reality.

—Qui-Gon Jinn, in *Star Wars*

Want to increase your life span by about four years, without having to exercise, quit smoking, or make any other life adjustments? You can do so by having a positive attitude, according to a study by Becca Leavy in a 2002 article in the *Journal of Personality and Social Psychology.*[1]

How does this concept play into the craft of business communication? It's very simple: we have to rethink how we send our messages. Think for a moment: how many times a day do you hear the word no? Or variations of that word, such as *can't, won't, couldn't* and so on? Probably lots. You probably use those words without truly even thinking about them, without realizing they are a part of your subconscious and therefore a part of your language.

Do they matter?

Yes. You may start your day in a good mood, with energy and goodwill toward those you work with, even toward the difficult people. But given enough messages with the variations of *no* in your day, the best mood deteriorates. It's as if you started your day with bright pretty watercolors on a clean canvas, but gradually the colors got murkier and murkier until they began to look like the dirty gray water that results if one dips the brush into the same water too often.

And you can be having a great day when someone else's gray water can splash all over it in the form of a negatively worded email. The sad part is that the sender may not have even known he was being negative. With simple attention to detail, you can ensure that you are never the bearer of

---

[1]Lamott, Anne (1994). *Bird by Bird.* New York, NY: Panthenon.

the dirty gray water. The first and easiest of these techniques is to become aware of how much you say what something isn't—and then replace it with what it actually is. Consider the following vagaries.

"That's not quite what I was looking for."

Okay, what exactly were you looking for? Tell the reader. That way, even if she was wrong, she knows. If you were looking for more statistics or more in-depth historical analysis, tell her. That way she knows how to proceed and give you what you wanted. That specificity creates a positive path. It gives hope and it gives confidence. She may have missed the mark here, but we aren't doomed forever. By telling her what you want—exactly— instead of what you don't want, you both win.

"It's not possible at this time."

Why? Tell her. Under what circumstances could it be possible? Maybe you can create those circumstances—or at least consider and maybe discuss with you whether creating a plan to achieve those circumstances is possible.

That discussion, by the way, also will do a whole lot for a positive at-titude and reaction even if the items we are discussing are unfavorable. By opening the conversation with at least telling her what is or could be, you honor her with the product of your mind. By being positive, you send the message that she is worth talking to instead of slamming the door in her face with the negatively worded statement. You keep the reader motivated.

Instead of telling her what you can't do, tell her what you can. In-stead of saying "I can't have this data to you until Friday," simply say, "I'll have this to you on Friday." Usually a clear definite positive statement such as this one will not be questioned; the other person sees you as will-ing to work with her and to get back to her in a reasonable time frame. The negatively worded comment, however, sends signals that *You are an imposition; you should be ashamed by asking me to do something when I am already so overworked.* Yech.In the rare case where the audience then questions why the due date is later than you preferred, you have the op-portunity to tell your reasons and create understanding. If having the information on Thursday is vital, by sharing your constraints you also give opportunity for her to help you remove some of those constraints so that she can have her data on Thursday. Maybe you have an earlier project requested for Thursday; if her need is so great, she can go to the earlier requester and negotiate which set of results should come first. You've created teamwork, or at least team communication.

Other versions of *no* pervade. For instance, think about the mindless "no problem" or "no worries" so many people say without thinking. These phrases, with which many late-night comics have skewered Gen Yers as using instead of a gracious and positive "you're welcome," sends a message of self-absorbed negativity. These phrases indicate that the user is independent and aloof, better than the other party, and while most requests are an intrusion—a problem or a worry—in this one case it isn't, but watch it. Columnist Kathleen Purvis of *The Charlotte Observer* states about servers who reply to "thank you" with "no problem" that she wants to reply, "as all customers over age 40 want to reply: 'You're right, it's no problem—it's your job.' She adds that she tips extra to those who say, "You're welcome."[2]

"You're welcome" has lasted hundreds of years, long before Gen Y, for a reason: it sends positivity. It sends a sense that you are not an ego maniac, caught up in self-absorption. It works.

Tone

Back when you were in middle school, most likely at some point one of your parents said to you, "Don't use that tone with me." If you were like most middle schoolers, you had no idea what your mom or dad was talking about. You just thought you were expressing your opinion.

Tone can be an inflection or it can be word choice.

If increasing the positive words in your message can change how well the message is received, think also about decreasing negative tone. How? You have to think about your own emotional state as you are trying to communicate. The middle schooler, for instance, may be unconsciously wanting to be treated less like a child, and as a result goes too far; in trying to avoid sounding like a small child, his tone overcompensates and becomes aggressive or belligerent.

[2]Lamott, Anne (1994). *Bird by Bird.* New York, NY: Panthenon.

Grownups who feel a lack of power can also overcompensate. If a little part of the brain is saying, "I'm the boss so they need to do what I say, even if I am afraid they won't, so I need to show them I'm the boss," that thought creeps in no matter how well constructed the message, it is going to have a haughty or belittling tone. Or that grownup can feel the same lack of power and retreat into fear, thinking "No one is going to listen to me anyway, and I am not treated well" or some other such thoughts. If that tape is running in the background of the conscious communication, the message is going to come out as a whine, a complaint, or some of that middle-school belligerence.

Note that none of these things that influence our tone is usually in our conscious minds. But being consciously aware of checking our emotions around the communication can help reduce negative tones.

My first mentor used to say to remember to HALT. She meant to avoid communicating something important when we were hungry, angry, lonely, or tired.

Very sage advice, since these are times when we are most likely to let those background emotions color our messages. Check in with your own feelings, and then take an objective look at how the feelings are controlling how you say the message. A collaborating tone always trumps a bossy one; kindness always goes farther professionally than sarcasm or a power trip.

Remember: it is not about you.

Role Reversal

Carl Rogers, the so-called father of industrial psychology, became famous for his approach to negotiations and conflict resolution.

One of the first steps of the Rogerian Technique, as it has come to be known, is to identify the issue without presenting your own side of the issue only. Then you do a quick role reversal, putting yourself in the recipient's shoes.

You describe how the issue looks from the other person's point of view, which should lead you to common ground and therefore a solution to the conflict. This same technique works in crafting messages. (We're back to the I box again.) Before you hit Send, put yourself in the reader's skin and roll around in there for a while. How does the message come across to him? What reactions show up? What emotions?

Are those answers the ones you want to show up in the receiver's inbox? If not, read on.

Asking Questions

One of Steven Covey's Seven Habits is to "seek to understand before you seek to be understood." While we discussed this concept a bit when we delved into the *tell, sell, join, consult* concepts, this habit also can go a long way in creating a positive atmosphere around your communication.

Most of us operate in silos, focusing on the screens in front of us as well as on our own to-do lists. We fall into that I mindset, which interestingly makes us increasingly less happy and less satisfied with what we are doing. Humans are by nature social creatures; we like to share ideas. We want other people to like us and be interested in us.

So asking questions about the message someone sent you can create a positive response—as long as we ask intelligent and other-focused questions. (Such things as "Are you out of your mind? What could you have possibly been thinking?" don't count as intelligent and other-focused questions; they are really all about our own judgment of the other person's thoughts or actions.)

Even simple questions that ask for clarification, data, or directions show that the other person's message has been heard. And yes, I am aware that we said a few chapters ago that the sender should have provided all these details. But we're talking about the receiver here. She needs to signal that not only has he gotten the message but is ready to run with it.

Think of this technique of asking questions as a football receiver getting the ball from the quarterback. While the best model for good communication is that the sender is a Tom Brady, sending the ball 70 yards down the field to land squarely in Dave Gronkowski's hands so that he can score, often what occurs is a flag football wannabe star who overestimates the power of his effort and has any number of possible receivers scrambling to see if they can catch anything at all.

So to create the communication teamwork and positive relationship, you reply. Although many responses that we may have to a situation as well as to a piece of communication seem as if they require a statement, in actuality we can phrase that statement as a question. For example:

You should take a look at the work that Cigna's doing in that area.

becomes

Have you looked at the work that companies such as Cigna have been doing in that area?

What's the difference? Well, in the first one, the perceived power levels are unequal; you may be offering a suggestion, but it comes across as if the person you are speaking to isn't quite as smart as you, or at least not able to think of what you just thought of. You may mean absolutely nothing by the statement other than offering a collaboration effort. But the receiver could possibly take offense. Especially in writing, without a spoken tone to adjust the message, this first statement could come across as arrogant and negative.

The second, however, by being a question, offers collaboration in an equal power manner. The receiver can say, *Yes, I have, and here's what I learned from doing so,*" which then carries on a conversation and allows that person to explain his thinking or ideas or findings. He can also say, *No, I haven't, and here's why,* which also allows him to express himself. Or he can say, *No, I haven't, but that's a great idea* or *No, I haven't; tell me why you think I should do so.*

In any of the possible responses to the question, the speaker operates out of position of feeling respected—which creates a positive aura around the communication itself. The two of you learn to work together. And the more you do, the closer you get to the Brady-Gronkowski model. Asking questions also allows other people to add to or develop your ideas. Perhaps you're in a meeting, and as you listen to what's being discussed, you become very convinced that members of another division need to be brought into the decision.

You can state that, as in

Before we make that decision, we need to include IT

—and run the risk of having someone else directly contradict your idea. They can do so simply out of a desire to move forward immediately, or out of a knee-jerk reaction to say no, or even just because it was you who brought up the idea. No matter what, once the contradiction is brought up, the idea is dead.

But if you say,

Is anyone else getting a strong sense that IT needs to be in on this decision?

then you give others a chance to chime in. Or they can ask you why you feel this way. Worst-case scenario is that they say no, in which case you can jump right in and offer your reasons for why you feel the way you do. The trick here is to ask questions to help critical thinking and to create a better decision. And that nearly always creates a positive, vibrant atmosphere.

Look for Context

Asking questions can also give you details that you may not ordinarily receive. For instance, perhaps your subordinate tells you about an instance where a client was less than happy with the work your team provided. While the subordinate may give you all the 5 W's and the WIFM as well as the headline up front just fine, by asking about the context in which the action occurred will give you a greater sense of understanding of the situation.

Instead of just saying,

We'll have to find a way to improve.

turning that into a question about context can open many avenues. Simply saying

I really want to understand all the details about the context in which this occurred. Can you describe everything to me, including where people were when they said what? That will help us both see ways we can improve on our service.

can reduce the subordinate's emotions around the event and allow a clearer picture of what can be done next.

What happens in each of these scenarios when we ask questions is that we pay attention to the other person. Yes, we learn information that can help us, which is an added bonus, and by seeking clarification we can often save ourselves hours of needless work. But the real benefit is that by allowing others to share their ideas and explain, we acknowledge that they themselves are of value. The questions, if worded in a positive manner, send the message that we see the others as equals, as people that we like to work with.

That message helps create positivity. And positivity creates results.

Seek the Yes

Even if you get a no, you can negate the negative atmosphere. While whining and sulking never works—and has residual long-term effects on later communication as well—seeking how the no could have become a yes can turn a negative atmosphere into a positive one. Asking what would need to occur before the answer could change can give you information that allows you to take control of the situation. Say, for example, you ask your boss for Friday off. She says no. By then asking, *Is there anything I could have done that would have turned that no into a yes?* you find out how to proceed next time—or whether proceeding on that path at all is worth your while.

Most of us tend to accept the negative so much that we never question why. In fact, we often anticipate the negative—to the point that we don't even bother to ask at all. Professor Emeritus Roy J. Lewicki of Ohio State offers an exercise that helps students see where they are creating their own negative atmospheres. Called "Collecting Nos," Lewicki tells his students to start asking for actions from others, then keeping a record. If the answer is no, the student is to then ask what he needed to do to turn that no into a yes.[3]

While the students do learn to ask for clarification and turn what could be a negative atmosphere into a positive one, what they learn as well is that communicators often don't ask enough. We often assume the answer will be no, so we don't ask. And we sit in the negativity, dissatisfied in a manner most of us can't put our fingers on. Students also learn from

---

[3]Lamott, Anne (1994). *Bird by Bird.* New York, NY: Panthenon.

Professor Lewicki's exercise that as their confidence in their own abilities to create positive atmospheres increases, their relationships become stronger. That alone can turn into opportunities.

After all, none of us likes working with Donna Downer. Seek the positive.

One More Thing

I am always struck anew about how much tone and listening go hand in hand. If we don't listen, we jump to conclusions that may not be right at all. And if we try to hurry people along, we often wind up at the wrong conclusion—which is why the *tell* approach so seldom works.

What happens when we try to hurry things along and don't truly listen is that we get in our own way; we listen in a biased manner, which then keeps us from practicing that empathy Carl Rogers talks about. It also keeps us from seeing the balance in life: we may be so irritated at Jenny, for instance, for asking for clarification on what we are sure was a perfectly worded message that our emotions keep us from questioning and trying to understand the breakdown in communications.

Instead, we try to discipline—which is what many of us call "*tell*" but isn't. Telling a person he needs to change isn't going to work. One tells facts. One sells a change. So if we haven't listened to see where the original process broke down, we can't give effective feedback. We think that everybody should see things our way, and woe be unto him who doesn't.

This phenomenon is known in negotiations theory as *illusion of consensus*. That means that we think we are right and that everyone agrees with us—or we think that everyone else thinks one way. Because we don't listen, we don't see that others are afraid to speak up; we go with the group in wanting to be right. Malcolm Gladwell, in his book *Blink*, and Thomas Gilgovich, in his book *How We Know What Isn't So*, address this phenomenon in great and entertaining detail; basically our unconscious does our thinking for us unless we listen for all possibilities. And our unconscious is one self-centered little critter.

We hear about the big screw-ups with illusion of consensus; New Coke, the Challenger and Columbia (not one but two exploded spaceships due to this illusion!) and the faulty General Motors switches. But they happen in micro situations as well: the manager who thinks that he has communicated but has not, and has only told *what* but not *how*; the exec who thinks that everyone is on board with his decisions only because he has created a culture of fear where no one is willing to speak up for fear of being fired; or the people who are too concerned about their positions to go against the prevailing thought.

My friend from grad school, who had been a Marine in Viet Nam, called this the "ANL syndrome," which stood for *Arrogant New Lieutenant*. In describing the ANL syndrome, he said, "If the guy came in telling us what to do without finding out why we had been doing something the way we had, or if he didn't tell us how to do it differently in a way we could use immediately, what would happen is that his men would wait for an opportune time, and then shoot him in the back." I hear examples of managers who are figuratively shot in the back weekly. Again, seek to understand. Listen.

Another example: My first mentor was a wonderful woman who knew truth that often I didn't want to hear. One of her statements was "Every action has a reaction, and those reactions have consequences." By that she meant that if we reacted—acted out of emotion rather than compassion—we usually created a mess. But if we stopped, listened, and looked at things from all angles dispassionately, we would make better choices and decisions.

Even if our decision wound up being the same as it would have been had before we listened, the manner in which we communicated that decision would always be better. She would then quote Garrison Keillor:

"Be kind to everyone, especially those who deserve it the least."

Listening is one small but powerful form of kindness. It creates positivity, yet it costs us so little.

To Sum Up

A woman I respect once said that her goal as a manager was to be someone that people were excited to work for. That to me says volumes. It says that she wants to be positive, enthusiastic, mentoring, and sympathetic. She wants to be someone who listens to her employees and who provides them with opportunities for growth that they want, not just that she shoves upon them.

It is a great goal—for all of us.

CHAPTER 11

Honor the Concrete

We are all hungry and thirsty for concrete images.
—Salvador Dali

Think about that word *concrete*. To most of us, the image the word conjures up is the gray-white stuff that makes up sidewalks. That image is a great way to understand the way the term is used in writing. Concrete is hard and durable. It can take all sorts of pressure and it remains the same. It holds things together. It can be painted, as in swimming pool bottoms, or drawn on, as with sidewalk chalk. It can be made into pillars several stories high, as in upright posts that suspend bridges over large rivers.

But one thing it never is: something else. Like concrete, good communication is almost always definite. Unfortunately, many of us are anything but. Consider the following example.

Try this experiment: Ask six people you know to describe what you mean by a "sports car." Chances are excellent you will receive six different answers: every color from white to black to red. You'll also get everything from a Mazda Miata to an antique Jaguar such as the one James Bond drove in the early movies to what is known as a muscle car—and even those may have to be explained. No one knows precisely what you mean by that term *sports car*. You know what you mean. No one else does.

Now while you may be thinking that you won't be using the term *sports car* at work, you will be using other similar terms. For instance, what does the phrase *make this report highly visible* mean? What does the term *at the end of the day* mean exactly? Truly at 5 p.m. today—or 7? Midnight? Or in the summation of the project? Are you using the term literally or symbolically? Do you even know what you mean?

What does *have a successful outcome* mean? How can, for instance, a department measure whether it's doing a good job if the instructions and the starting point of the goals aren't spelled out in clear terms? A department may *say we want to increase our profits by 16 percent by the end of next quarter.* Well, that sounds good. But specifically how? Does it do so by laying off employees? Selling more products? Increasing the prices on the products you already have?

To be clear, you have to use words that are unmistakable in their meanings. You don't use words that allow you—or anyone else—to weasel out of what the message was intended to convey. This concept is called *being concrete.* It means when I say *you need to sit in the chair*, you know what I mean by the word *chair.* You know it's not a sofa, you know it's not a rolling stool, you know it's not the floor. You know exactly what I mean. You don't get a chance to say, "But hey, I thought you meant...."

And while we may think that being concrete is another form of being aggressive, in reality it is not.

> Being concrete allows the other person the respect and ease of being able to know exactly what you mean and not have to guess.

Your receiver can then respond with her own ideas—and neither of you waste time having to redo your conversation once you find out that you are talking about different things.

Abstraction: The Enemy of Simplicity

The opposite of concrete is *abstract.* An *abstraction* is a concept whose definition changes with each person who hears the word. How does one define a word? Think about it. In some cases, such as defining a table, you and your 60 closest friends would all agree on what a table should be. You may imagine different sizes, but in general you all have in this case a concrete definition: a table has a flat top that is supported by legs.

But let's say you and only two of those friends decide you want to go out on a Friday and have a good time. Chances are very strong that all three of you have varying ideas of what a good time should be. That's because the concept of *a good time* is an abstraction. And when you start having multiple meanings of a message, the confusion begins.

Some people argue that being concrete limits possibilities. On the contrary: being concrete gives everyone the same starting point. It doesn't create confusion at the starting gate. A table, for example, can be made out of wood, stone, plexiglass—the list goes on. It can have three legs, four legs, one leg. Ask any college design major: having a concrete, agreed-on starting place expands creativity, not limits it. Without that agreed-upon starting place, you have no idea where to begin.

Being concrete, then, is allowing creativity. It also allows both simplicity and details. If I tell you that the sports car I mean is a 1961 Jaguar XKE, creating the image in your mind is simple. You can then add details: black cowhide leather seats, a teakwood dash, and a holder for one martini—shaken, not stirred.

Remember: simplicity does not mean simple-minded. By concentrating on the essence, the core or main idea of something, and seeing it as it is, one sees precision and details. By stripping away the emotional baggage, emotional reactions, and attachments that we often unconsciously place on words and ideas, we see objectively, which allows us to see the word as it is. Therefore, it becomes what it is, not what our emotions want it to be.

Take, for instance, a Coach handbag or a designer pair of jeans. To many, having the little symbol on our possessions sends a message to ourselves—and hopefully others—that we are superior in some way; we have enough money or enough style or enough economic or social class to own one of these things. But if we strip down the symbols and emotional attachment, we see the item as it is: a leather bag to carry items in, or a stitched-together piece of denim that covers our bottom halves. We can then examine the workmanship, the quality of the materials, even the design of the item. Does it have a working zipper, for instance? Are the pockets in alignment?

Once we see the details, our emotional reaction to the word changes. In most cases, it diminishes, which helps with our own ability to see clearly not only the word, but the entire idea. Having that touch of "what will people think of me?" either consciously or unconsciously blurs the ability for both the sender and the receiver of the communication to see the idea as it is.

So while our emotions may want the word or idea to be a reflection of our own worthiness, removing those in Zen fashion allows us to think critically about the item and examine its worth on its own merits. We no longer see it as a reflection of us.

Just as we did with the designer item, by stripping away that reflection of self and touch of solipsism in our communication, we see the details and possibilities that one misses with large words, large sentences, and pomposity. Consider, for instance, the confusion that arises from a many commonly used business communication phrase: *As soon as possible*—what actually does that mean? Possible for you? Under what circumstances? To the extent we ignore what? If 3:00 is as soon as I can devote time to the task, is that early enough for you? Why or why not? And why for that matter do you and your time requests matter more than the ones I already have?

Implied in the *as soon as possible* is *I need it and do it soon or else*. It is one of the ultimate in self-absorbed messages; even if the writer consciously means that the other person can take his time. Implied unconsciously in the message is *it's really all about me; I didn't check with you to see what you had going on or what you might need; I just need it*. Without taking the time to clarify and be concrete, the sender of the *as soon as possible* message comes across as a self-centered aggressive despot, no matter what his intentions were in sending that message. He falls back into that I box we've been referring to all along.

Inside all of us is a sulky self-centered teenager. Depending on the day and the day's events, that sulky teenager can be buried deep under the covers or be sitting up front of our reactions, arms folded and just itching for an argument. If the teenager is awake and butting into our professional demeanor one day, and we receive a message that said something has to be done as soon as possible—oh, my. If we are in the middle of another large project, that inner teenager would probably put the *as soon as possible* item on the back burner just because she doesn't like her autonomy affronted. Your *as soon as possible* now means as soon as she feels like it, no matter what your needs are. It's all about her, you know.

However, for the writer, the issue and the request may mean he needs information that is dire and has to be supplied within the next half an hour in order for the writer to continue to do his work. The use of the

comment *as soon as possible* doesn't convey that message. If the writer had taken the time to explain simply and clearly *I need the information to 10 minutes in order to complete a report the boss wants in two hours,* the teenager probably would have paused what she was doing, sent the information, and moved on. Both would have been happy, secure in simplicity and clarity of the request. Even the teenager couldn't come up with an argument about that one. (Well, maybe….). But most people don't take the time to realize that simple and clear is best. They know what they mean; therefore they convey what it means to them, without thinking of clarifying and simplifying for others to understand.

Being concrete means thinking about the many ways your words can be taken. You know what you mean, but if you are in that I box, you will usually neglect to see that others don't think the same way you do. Even something as simple as confirming to a coworker who's offered to pick up lunch for the office that you would like a salmon bagel may result in something other than what you intended. You may mean a plain bagel with salmon cream cheese; she may see that the shop offers bagels with smoked salmon on them and buy that. Or you may wind up with a plain bagel that just happens to have salmon flavoring baked inside it. Regardless, to ensure that you get what you want, you have to think about how someone else could take your words.

While that sulky teenager in the sender wants to jump up right now and yell, "Why should I have to be the one who has to do everything?" he needs to be aware that by making sure what is said is concrete, he is actually gaining time. He doesn't have to go back and redo something because it wasn't done right the first time. He also doesn't have it hanging over his head, coming back to haunt and torment him (like yesterday's forgotten homework now piled up on top of today's). Most importantly, he gets what he wants. In a weird Machiavellian fashion, making sure that he is concrete winds up benefitting him. It's the ultimate self-satisfying tool, because the end does justify the means.

Can being concrete really be that important? Consider the following.

A few years ago a young woman sued her employer. For over four years, she had been receiving on her performance evaluations the comment that her communication skills "needed to be improved." So when she first received one of these mentions and comments, she set about to do something about it. She took advanced software class and passed with distinction.

Yet on the next evaluation she also received the same comment; this time she enrolled into Toastmasters. Six months later she received the same comment, although she was making progress and felt that her public speaking skills in front of a group had improved. So she then took a business writing course, in which she made an A. Still, at the next performance evaluation, she received the same comment.

Frustrated, she went to HR. All they could tell her was yes, that her "communication skills still required work." Although she had done everything she could think of to do, she then decided that she was being discriminated against in some way. In her mind, she had addressed everything that *communication skills* meant. What emerged at the hearing after she filed suit was that the Boston-based company felt that her southern accent made her inappropriate for any form of promotion. They felt that they had sent that message clearly through the comment that her communication skills needed to be improved. Yet at no time did she understand that was what they meant. She had fixed everything that "communication skills" meant to her.

But the lack of concreteness in the company's directives backfired on them. While, as her boss explained in court, the company had hoped to avoid any kind of hurt feelings they felt would have occurred by expressing that her southern accent did not meet with Boston standards, in fact they were found guilty of discrimination and of failure to provide clear performance goals and directives. She won a sizeable sum and also left the company for another firm where she was hired at 50 percent more than the first company was paying her. By the use of abstractions, and lack of concrete communication, the Boston-based company not only paid a large sum of money in fines and lost goodwill in the news and press. It also lost a highly qualified and willing employee whose only fault was that she did not understand that her employers disliked her accent.

Had the company's management not been so worried about how to avoid hurting this woman's feelings and therefore worded its message in a convoluted abstract form, it probably could've found a way to be positive and nurturing while delivering the message. In the court hearing, the young woman stated that her feelings would not have been hurt had the company said "most of our administrators are based in Boston, and they feel that your accent will hurt your progress." She was far more hurt by the fact that they refused to tell her concretely what she needed to do. Their wording wasted her time and wasted her potential, which was far more damaging than hearing that administration wanted her to work on her accent.

Connotations: Another Trap Waiting to Happen

So let's say that you've been very careful to choose words with clear meanings, and you're pretty sure that you've been concrete in your message. You may think you are ready to hit that send button, but wait. There's more.

Words have denotations, which is what we were talking about with abstractions. But they also have connotations.

A denotation is the dictionary meaning. A connotation is the emotional baggage that meaning brings along for the ride.

For instance, take the two words *senator* and *politician*. If you look them up in the dictionary, you will find almost the exact same definition, with the only difference being that the senator holds a specific office whereas the politician can hold several. But think of the images these two words create: for *senator*, we immediately think of someone upstanding and honorable, doing his best to represent the people who elected him, selfless and deliberate in all actions, a staunch pillar of our American government. When the media said that John Edwards had disgraced his role as a senator, it was referring to that image.

Now think of what comes immediately to mind when you hear the word *politician*. For most of us, we immediately get a sense of something not quite right, someone self-serving and glib-tongued, glad-handing, and slightly repulsive. Yet the two words by denotation are almost exactly the same.

All of us have these immediate knee-jerk reactions to words floating around in the backs of our minds, eager to come forth whenever their names are called. Being aware of those emotional reactions and keeping the wrong ones at bay is crucial in communication. Perhaps you describe an employee as *sensitive*. You may mean that she is pretty good at picking up the small details and nuances of the daily work processes, that she is highly emotionally intelligent. And you would be using the word in its proper concrete manner, as in *She is aware and uses her senses to notice things that others do not.*

But by that one use, without being aware of the connotation baggage, you could unwittingly send the message that she is self-absorbed, easily hurt and offended, and emotional. After all, that's what the connotation could suggest to others. And by that one small use of words, you could doom her career forever.

Not All Words Are the Same

In his poem *Ulysses*, Tennyson wrote that the title character was "a part of all that I have met." And that fact is true with our understanding of words—both their denotations and connotations.

All of us have a mental body of reference for words and their images. Some of these are taught by our experiences while some are a part of our upbringing. Children who were old enough to understand what was happening on 9/11 have a different frame of reference from those who are too young to have been aware. Popular culture also plays a part in how we process information and words; those who grew up listening to the Grateful Dead and the BeeGees will have different references in that mental box than someone who was a teenager in the age of Grunge.

So a *supportive boss* to a Baby Boomer may mean one who allows the employee to work independently and who rewards her financially. But that same concept of *supportive boss* to a Gen Xer may mean a boss who provides training and sets up the employee for quick career moves. The Gen Yer sees that *supportive boss* as one who provides very detailed instructions and spends a significant amount of time with the employee—what the Gen Xer would see as micromanaging and what the Baby Boomer would see as coddling.

Those differences reveal themselves in slang as well as in informal language. Be aware that different generations have different connotations for words. When a Gen Yer says that an idea is really sick, he means it's terrific. Yet a Baby Boomer or Gen Xer, told that the idea is sick, will either immediately wonder how the idea shows obscenity or perversion.

People from different areas of the country also have different connotations as well as denotations for certain words. To someone who grew up in Ohio, a Coca Cola or Pepsi is a soda, while in other parts of the country a soda is an ice cream concoction with seltzer water. A toboggan in New England is a sled; in the South, it's a close-fitting knit cap. A tag sale in the West is the same as a garage sale or attic sale elsewhere. The glove box is also the glove holder or glove compartment (although most of us put everything but gloves in this recessed storage area in the car dashboard).

Although differences are fun to notice, be aware of what is known as *reactive devaluation*, which describes the tendency to automatically judge a person as inferior to you or pretentious because he uses a different term than you do for the same idea. You devalue that person unconsciously because his use of words is different. Being aware of that phenomenon can save you hours of misunderstanding and eliminate possible bias, both in you and in your audience.

In Summary

A great deal of embarrassment, pain, and wasted time can be avoided if we take the time to pause before we spoke. What makes sense to us doesn't necessarily make sense to others—yet the whole point of communication is for other people to see our ideas. Often we take for granted that our words are concrete, when they are anything but. Investing some time into investigating just how other people interpret words before you communicate with them can yield big results. In other words, be concrete.

CHAPTER 12

Honor the Definite (or How to Clean Up Your Act)

The difference between the right word and the almost right word is the difference between lightning and a lightning bug.

—Mark Twain

Are we ever definite about anything? Ask me if I can have lunch with you a week from today and I will most likely say, "Probably." Ask me if I think I have enough money saved to retire when I turn 70, and I most likely will say, "I hope so." Heck, even in these examples I am using *will most likely*. Life happens, and with the amount of information that comes at us these days, being definite on issues may be difficult. But you can help clear up some of the haze by being definite in your word choices.

A *definite* word is a word whose meaning is clear. Grammatically, a definite word has a clear antecedent (word it refers to) and creates a clear image. An *indefinite* word forces the receiver of the message to guess what you mean.

Indefinite Nouns

Indefinite nouns occur when we use imprecise, catch-all words to try to describe thoughts we haven't clearly identified. Some of the more common indefinite nouns include *things, stuff, trouble, activity, efforts,* and *someone*.

If you write a sentence such as *you need to do several things before your project is complete,* you really haven't formulated a clear idea. The other person has to ask you, or you have to think about, what those things actually are. Does he need to check with IT to make sure the bandwidth is big enough? Does he have to test out the speakers and microphones? Does he have to prepare an agenda, make sure everyone who needs to be at the meeting is at the meeting, send out the links, test the links, test everything that is recording? How about sending out information on how to test the connection? In other words, what do you mean by *things?*

Avoiding indefinite nouns requires discipline of mind. You can't just send a flick-of-your-hand- and-promise-to-think-about-it-later message; you have to be clear about your own thoughts before you send out that message. While you may be thinking *I don't have the time to clarify those things*, you simply do not have the time not to. Without taking the time to think through something before you use a word, you run the risk of being misunderstood. And that itself will cause a huge expenditure of time just to clarify what you should've done in the first place. Again, a little investment on the frontend yields big returns in time and clarity on the backend.

That's in the micro world. In the macro world, using indefinite nouns can cause huge misunderstandings. At best, using them can delay action. At worst, using them can create rifts between groups or create anger and discomfort in a large section of the population. We have to be careful that we define what we mean. If we aren't talking about the same thing, we make no progress.

For example, some general concepts also become indefinite nouns. How do we define *happiness? Irritation?* But the more important indefinite nouns are ones we use to talk about larger concepts and absolutes. Take the word *poverty* for instance. Does poverty just mean poor? How do you define *poor?* Is what is considered poor in rural Nebraska the same as you define *poor* in San Francisco? Does *poor* mean a certain income level? A certain group? The word *poor* often serves as a code for a squirrel's nest of issues related to race, social class, opportunity, cultural values, and regional identity. It serves as an emotional trigger for many people, and quite often we are swayed by our own definition of the word rather than a rational, clear definition of what the person who used the word is talking about.

Sometimes we also are deliberately deceived as the user intends for us to have an emotional reaction rather than a logical reaction to this word. The same effect happens with imprecise nouns such as *family, religious, conservative, liberal.* Can you be a conservative and still support what many would consider to be liberal causes? By *family* do you mean the nuclear family? Extended family? If the majority of America is no longer a two-parent household consisting of one male and one female parent, can we define the word by that concept?

And if we talk about *family values*, doesn't each family value something different? We may value SEC football in my family while your family values ACC basketball. We need to be specific. If you're conservative, does that mean you don't support issues about the environment? One may think that someone who composts everything, recycles, uses green energy, and is a careful steward of the earth would not be labeled *conservative*. But how is that different from being a conservationist? Before choosing your words, do some clear thinking about what you actually mean. Having specific and concrete ideas makes progress as well as understanding much clearer.

Indefinite Modifiers

Modifiers can also be indefinite or definite. You may know what you mean—or you may not. If someone is very successful, just how successful is he? How do you measure success? If you need considerable effort to finish a project, how much exactly do you need? What you may perceive as *considerable* may to me be *trivial* or *insignificant*. But unless I explain to you what my definition of trivial is, we have a flyby—our ideas never connect because we really don't know for sure what the other person means.

Some other indefinite modifiers include the word *really*; if I worked *really hard* on the project, how do I define really, in time, effort, and thought? Or if I work *very* hard, again how much time, effort, thought, etc. did I put into my effort? Other indefinite modifiers include *professional* and *managerial*. Effective companies spell out exactly what their definition of professional is. What precisely does one need to do to be managerial?

Indefinite Pronouns

Quick: what's a pronoun?

Pronouns replace a noun. So if I am talking about Marty, and I say, *Marty is the manager at Best Buy; he will make sure you get the right laptop cord*, the word *he* is the pronoun. It replaces *Marty*.

Pronouns are very helpful words. They keep us from boring people to death—can you imagine what that sentence above would sound like if I didn't use the pronoun? *Marty is the manager at Best Buy; Marty will make sure you get the right laptop cord.* I'd wind up sounding like some 1950s advertising jingle. All you would hear is the repetition of his name; you'd miss the point of my sentence.

So far so good. Next comes the tricky part. Some pronouns are called *demonstrative pronouns.* They point out particular people or things. We have only four of them in the English language: *these, that, this,* and *those.* And here is where the problems begin. Suppose I am having lunch. Today my lunch consists of a salami sandwich, blueberries, yogurt, homemade hummus, and ice cream. My friend walks up, looks at my lunch, and says, "I want some of that." Some of what? I have five things in front of me. Which one do you want? All five? Just the hummus? What?

Anyone who has ever had to deal with a tearful two-year-old crying, "Want that!" knows the situation. Because you aren't sure what she's referring to, every effort you make seems to make the situation worse. Guess what: the same lack of clarity and making things worse occurs daily in business writing. When we aren't clear as to what word we want our pronoun to refer to is, we have what is known as an *indefinite pronoun.*

Indefinite pronouns are the near misses of life.

The good news: making your pronouns definite is easy. First you have to approach the concept logically: a *pronoun* replaces a noun. Although we have several types of pronouns in the English language, an *indefinite* pronoun error usually occurs in the use of personal pronouns.

Now think logically: if something *replaces* something else, don't you have to have that something else first? In other words, you have to have a noun before you can replace it with a pronoun. An *indefinite* pronoun occurs when you don't have that noun. We aren't definite about what the writer means, so the use becomes *indefinite.*

For example:

It is this process that makes our beer unique. [Apologies to Coors, but an error is an error.]

The pronoun in this sentence is *it*. But does the word "it" replace anything? No. What the pronoun refers to is the word "process." But process comes *after* the pronoun, so the usage is incorrect. And the pronoun is indefinite.

Or look at this example:

They say that Hurricane Hanna will hit Savannah.

Who is "they"? We don't know. So the pronoun is indefinite.
Or this example:

This is what I want.

What is "this"? This what? We don't know. So the error is indefinite.
To fix this problem, ask yourself, "What does the pronoun refer to?" Then use the answer as you revise. So the first example then becomes

This process makes our beer unique. [See how I not only cut the "it is" but the "that"? Not every "that" needs to be cut, by the way; relative pronouns are necessary in certain situations. But here we didn't need the that.]

The second example would now read

Weather forecasters say that Hurricane Hanna will hit Savannah.

And the third one becomes

This format is what I want.

See how making sure your pronouns are definite makes your writing clearer?

More on Making Your Pronouns Definite: You Have to Make Them Get along With Each Other

To be clear, you need to make your nouns and the pronouns that refer to those nouns *agree*. To agree means the pronoun has to be the same gender and number as the noun; that way your message is clear. Yet we mess this one up often as well.

Take a look at the following. What's wrong here?

When the patient is on time and prepared, the appointment they are scheduled for goes more smoothly.

Or here?

Duke Energy has raised their rates. They want to make more money.

Test of logic: How many people is they? More than one, right? How many people is one organization? Well, this one is tricky. While the organization is comprised of many different people, sometimes into the thousands of people, it is still one organization. It is still one entity. In other words, it is *one*.

More logic: can one equal more than one? Absolutely not.

But in grammar, the rule states that the pronoun that replaces a noun has to agree with the noun in number. That means it has to be the same number as the noun is. So in the first example, *the patient* is one. But *they* is more than one. So the sentence has an agreement error.

That same error occurs in the second sentence. Duke Energy is one corporation; therefore, it is singular. It is one. The pronoun that refers to Duke Energy in the second sentence is our old friend *they*. If we use that *they*, then we have an agreement error.

So what? Does it matter?

It does. Although some of us may be inclined to dismiss the value of having these two items agree, think for a moment about what we lose when we pitch this rule out the window. First, we lose clarity. The listener (or reader) may be listening with only half his mind focused on your words—something that happens often. And he may hear that *they* and think he has lost somehow the thread of what you were saying. By losing that one small tight thread, we risk losing the whole intent of the message. If the listener starts wondering who *they* is and doesn't listen to the rest of your message, you've lost the whole shooting match.

Second, we lose a little of our professional image. As we have discussed before, professionalism is far more than being able to wear a suit and use big words; overusing big words will hurt your image, but misusing the small words will cause serious harm. Just as your mom told you to always wear clean underwear in case you were in a wreck because you never knew who would see you, I'm telling you to always make your pronouns and nouns agree. You never know who will be listening to or reading your words—and who will notice if those words don't agree. Part of professionalism is being able to put your best communication forward. You don't want something like an agreement error to mar your image.

OK, You Say. You Get It. What About Political Correctness?

But if you make the noun and pronoun agree, you may argue, you have to use *he*. And you want to be politically correct. You don't want to offend the women in the world—a smart move, by the way.

Zen teaches us that often the simplest way is the best way. When we try to make things more complicated, we find ourselves in our own way, and therefore look for an easy way out—hence the *they*. But Zen also teaches us that in simplicity we must also find order. And order requires acknowledgment of basic truths, such as the fact that one does not equal more than one.

So how do you fix the issue? For the first sentence, you can do one of three things:

- You can alternate between *he* and *she*.
- You can make the noun plural, as in *the patients*.
- Or you can go ahead and use *he*. People will forgive your masculine-dominant pronoun a lot more easily than they will forgive an unclear sentence.

So let's go back to the second sentence:

Duke Energy has raised their rates. They want to make more money.

To fix the sentence, first find your noun; in this case, it is *Duke Energy*. Now ask yourself how many the noun is. In this case, it is one. That one is known as a *collective noun*, which means it is one thing comprised of many; all of those employees are *collected* into one entity.

A collective noun is an *it*. So you use *it* and *its*:

Duke Energy has raised its rates. It wants to make more money.

Simple.

The Indefinite They: Who Are These They People, and Why Are They Making My Life Difficult?

At the risk of becoming the grammar police, at this point I have to talk about those *they* people. Who are they? We hear all the time something such as "*They* say it is going to rain" or variations. Yet we still don't know

who *they* are. *They* has become an American vernacular, a sort of catch-all phrase to refer to a vague unclear person or group of persons not totally identified. Using that generic unidentified *they* allows us to be imprecise and vague—not at all what we want to be.

> Lack of clarity is the enemy of Zen. Precision, clarity, and accuracy may all sound like legal terminology that is as distasteful as boiled grub worms, but in actuality, they are the basics of ease and simplicity.

To help your communication reach that inner peace and ease, what we need to do is simplify. *They say*—who's *they*? Answer the question. Was *they* the meteorologist on television, your uncle Phil who felt the rain in his bones, or a report in the online newspaper? To be clear, we need to be aware of how we speak. *They* becomes therefore not only another of those indefinite pronouns but sneakily one the biggest clarity stealers of all time.

The clearest way for us to communicate the message, one in which the other person knows exactly what we are talking about, is to just replace the *they*. So replacing the they with the answer to *Who do you mean by that they again?* gives us "the forecast says it's going to rain," which is a lot clearer.

The Indefinite It

Take a look at the following sentence:

> *If a company-wide method is put in place, it gives deliverers a blue print.*

Now tell me: what's (or who's) *it?*

In this sentence, the word *it* refers to *the company-wide method.* Nothing is grammatically wrong here.

But something structurally is wrong. Read that sentence aloud. Do you hear the looseness of the sentence? By *looseness,* we mean that the manner in which the sentence is constructed allows the reader to do one of a few things as he reads. She can slur all the words together, without any real rhythm or emphasis, which then allows her to say or read the words without attaching much meaning to them or internalizing them. Or she can read the words all in the same monotone, which has the same non-internalizing effect. In essence, the looseness of the sentence construction makes the content as bland as yesterday's French fries, kind of gooey and not of any real enjoyment or value.

What made the sentence loose? The pronoun.

Let's go back to the Zen concept of simplicity. We keep only what we need. Sometimes we need a pronoun, as we did in the sentences about the patient and Duke Energy. But often we do not; we just add in the pronoun because we didn't give enough due forethought and clarity to our own thoughts as we wrote them down or spoke them. In the sentence about the company-wide methods, we don't need a pronoun at all. We need to tighten and cut unnecessary parts.

So:

If a company-wide method is put in place, it gives deliverers a blue print.

becomes

A company-wide method gives deliverers a blue print.

See how this simple change makes the sentence stronger and clearer?

Ridding the World of *there*

Another of the great clarity stealers is the word *there*. The word *there* means location, as in *The way to Rome is over there* (in contrast to being *here*).

But so many of us use *there* as a slipped-clutch catch-all to start a sentence. The result is a reader or listener whose mental focus is jolted and thrown off balance, which in turn cuts off her best focus on the speaker's idea.

Look, for instance, at the following:

There is a lot of stress and pressure placed on group leaders daily, weekly and annually.

What's wrong with the sentence? The *there* (but you knew that, didn't you, because we are talking about *there.)* But what's wrong with it? Remember that *there* means location.

Read the sentence again. Do you see any location mentioned in that sentence? In fact, does the sentence have anything at all to do with location?

It does not. You can't answer *where* by reading the sentence. Therefore, it has nothing to do with location. The *there is* simply isn't needed. It's a lazy way of starting the sentence. We tried to make *there* a subject, but because it doesn't refer to anything, it isn't a noun. It's an indefinite.

So the "subject" is an indefinite but not a pronoun or a noun. Therefore, it can't take a verb, even if the writer has tried by tacking on that bland little *is*. The *there is* is meaningless and empty. It adds no value; in fact, all it does is take up valuable space in the reader's mind. It needs to go. So to fix the sentence, first ask yourself who is doing the placing. You don't have an answer in this sentence, so you will have to guess—just as the reader or listener of this sentence will have to do, and chances are good that the guesses will be something quite different from what you as the writer intended.

What you have in this instance is what is known as hidden passive; that means you have an accusation but no facts to back it up. So who is doing the placing? The boss? The job? The employees themselves? You have to answer the question. Who is placing? For the sake of example, let's say that the manager is placing unnecessary stress. Therefore,

> *There is a lot of stress and pressure placed on group leaders daily, weekly and annually.*

becomes

> *The manager places a lot of stress and pressure on group leaders daily, weekly and annually.*

See how much clearer the revised version of the sentence is? Hear how much stronger and—ahem—more professional the revised version sounds?

One Last Sneaky *there*

Look at this sentence:

There is a list that tells you what to do.

This one's easy. Is location what matters here? Nope. What matters is that the list tells you what to do. So shift your subject. Cut the *there is* totally and let the word *list* be your new subject. You will have to cut the word *that*, but because you used *that* only as a ballast against the unnecessary weight of the *there is*, you can cut it happily.

One Closing Thought

In a world where someone gives us a present that is *almost* what we wanted, gives us information that is *close to* what we needed, or opportunities that we *nearly* saw before it was too late, we need to be definite when we can.

Check your nouns, your modifiers, and your pronouns. Your listener and readers will thank you.

CHAPTER 13

Respect the Flow (or How to Use Transitions)

Flow is hard to achieve without effort. Flow is not 'wasting time.'
—Mihaly Csikszentmihalyi

Look up any website that sells posters of inspirational quotes and you will see that many have background pictures of flowing water. Humans naturally crave flow. Whether it's because as some scholars have claimed that we all want to return to the sea, or we've been programmed to think of water as soothing, images of flowing water do seem soothing.

Flowing communication can also be soothing and satisfying, as long as it follows some rules. Mere gushing doesn't flow; it overwhelms and makes the reader recoil. A huge burst of words, usually without paragraphing or punctuation, repels.

Flow is gentle but firm, clear, and always controlled. Flow is energized and energizing, full of focus. And getting some flow is not difficult.

The Opposite of Flow, or How to Recognize What You Don't Want

If you have ever driven a car with manual transmission, you will be familiar with the expression *a slipped clutch*. Manual transmission requires that the driver push in the clutch while changing the gears in the car; an automatic transition car, in contrast, does this transition for you. But when drivers learn to drive a car with manual transmission, they find a phenomenon happening all too often: it's called the slipped clutch. That means that the driver can't move the gears in time to sync with the clutch.

This lack of sync usually results in a car that bounces up and down, jolting the occupants of the car.

This slipped clutch phenomena happens in writing as well. It occurs when the writer uses a construction that will jolt the reader, mainly because he doesn't have the gear in place to continue his idea. When you drive the car, you need to have the gear in place to keep going forward. When you write a sentence, you need to have your idea in place to keep going forward.

But many things can mess up that smooth transition. And one of them is the inclusion of useless words and phrases that becomes the slipped clutches of writing. Let's take a look at what that actually means. The first chief offender in the slipped clutch of writing and life is the phrase *there is* or *there are*. By starting a sentence with *there is* or *there are*, you slip the clutch. We've already talked about how these phrases disconnect the idea that you are writing about and therefore give the reader a chance to jump along and fall off the path.

Consider: *There is a trash can in the corner of the room.* Where is it? *In the corner of the room.* Do you need that *there is*? Most likely not; all it indicates is location. If you simply cut it, you have a stronger sentence, a clear sentence, and you keep your reader on the path. *The trash can is in the corner of the room.* By eliminating excess, we find simplicity. And in simplicity once again is clarity—along with a smooth ride.

In communication, transition tells the reader or listener what to be aware of next. Like pioneers hunting for the next signpost that tells us which way to go on the Oregon Trail, transitions allow others to follow our random ideas by establishing logical connections between sentences, paragraphs, and sections of our message.

Transitions also fuse together ideas to become one thought. By doing so, you enhance the experience for the receiver of the message. You give what is known as *fluidity*, or *flow*, to your communication. The opposite of flow is commonly called *being choppy*, or *being abrupt*. In this state, your receiver has to jump from ledge to ledge like some character in a Mario Brothers game, worried about how to connect to the next idea. In flow, she can float along, taking time to notice the details of your message and the nuances. She takes in more of the message since she doesn't have to work so hard to try to put the individual thoughts into a cohesive whole.

A transition can be a simple word, sentence, phrase, or even a whole transitory paragraph. Whichever you choose, the transition device will in some manner either directly summarize or reflect what you have just said by reminding the reader in some manner of the previous content. It then will give a tiny preview of what is to come. In other words, transitions are great for helping you help audiences who aren't exactly paying 100 percent attention. By using the transitory device, you rope them back to the subject at hand.

You can adapt transitory devices to suit whatever needs you have in making your writing flow. Want to use a word in one spot and then a phrase in another? Do it.

Convinced? As the old Ronco TV ads used to say, *wait—there's more.*

Basic Transition, or Simple Words of Direction

The hardest part of adding transitions to your work is deciding on the logical relationship between the ideas. You have to take a step back and think, "How is this idea connected to the next?" Luckily, once you have done so, then you have a list of options from which to choose.

If you decide, for instance, that your ideas are connected logically by time, you can use such transitory devices between them as *after, afterward, as a result, at last, before, currently during, earlier, immediately, later, meanwhile, now, previously, recently, simultaneously, subsequently, then,* or *while.*

Notice the difference that the transitions make in the paragraphs below:

John woke up late on Monday. His alarm had been set to a later time than usual. He had to hurry through dressing. He had to eat his breakfast. He dropped oatmeal on his tie. He missed his carpool.

Hear the choppiness? The same paragraph, this time with transitions, makes for a smoother ride:

John woke up late on Monday. Previously, his alarm had been set to a later time than usual. As a result, he had to hurry through dressing and simultaneously had to eat his breakfast. While doing so, he dropped oatmeal on his tie. Meanwhile, he missed his carpool.

Hear the difference? In the second, you can put yourself in John's place and empathize with his situation. In the first, you just hear ideas.

If your logical connection is sequence, you can use such transitory devices as *first, second, third* and so on, *finally, moreover, also, in addition, furthermore, next, then,* or *after.* If your logical connection is example, you can use *for example, for instance, in particular, specifically,* or *to illustrate.*

If your logical connection is comparison or contrast, the transitory devices available to you include *similarly, not only but also, in comparison, also, in the same way, just as, in the same manner, although, but, while, however, in contrast, on the other hand, in spite of, nevertheless, on the contrary, yet, still,* and *in contrast.*

Have a cause and effect relationship? Use devices such as *therefore, thus, as a result, consequently,* or *accordingly.* If the logical relationship is that the second idea supports the first, use devices such as *in addition, additionally, furthermore, also, equally important, moreover,* and *as well.* (Good old *and* works here too, but use it sparingly.)

You can signal to your audience that you are summarizing or concluding a section by using such words as *in conclusion, finally, to summarize, in summary, to conclude,* or *thus.* Heck, you can even show position and place via transitions, as in *beyond, before, behind, in front of, next to, alongside of, above, in back of,* and *nearby.*

Adding transitions, my friends, is not only a cool thing to do for your audience. It's actually a lot of fun.

Transitions Between Sentences

Using transitory words aren't the only form of transition, however. Humans like clear and easy transition between ideas. We may think in a jumbled mess, hodgepodge of stuff lying in the middle of the box of our brains, but we don't like inheriting someone else's mess.

Part of the problem of being human is being able to organize all of that stuff and thought. Ellen Langer of Harvard has spent almost 40 years demonstrating in her research that most people don't think; they react emotionally and call it thought. And, when they put that emotional reaction in front of someone else and call it communication, they are confused when it is misunderstood. That's where having an idea of transition between sentences helps.

A good sentence is one distinct thought. The writer has taken the time to sort through, organize, and arrange thought into a manner in which someone else can see that thought quickly and clearly. One idea equals one thought.

The issue here is that most of us don't put the appropriate points in the appropriate spots of the sentence. So when we think one sentence's main thought is clear, we find that it isn't always clear in structure. Observe:

Thousands of outdoor winter sports enthusiasts descend upon Aspen every winter.

The sentence seems clear, doesn't it? But what we don't know is what exactly the writer intended. Is he talking about Aspen in the winter? Just Aspen? The number of ski enthusiasts? Enthusiasts themselves? We don't know where the writer is going with that idea, so the next step and logical thought is lost. Our brains stand without a map, no GPS inside, blindly waiting to see in the wilderness where the next possible path for thought might be.

Most people read what is known as a Z formation; they start at the beginning with all good intentions of paying attention, scan to the end of the line, and then perhaps drop to the end of the sentence to pay attention to the last word.

But what if the main part of the thought to the sender is in that middle part of the sentence that the reader has just scanned? Then his message, his true thought, has been lost.

The reality is that while most of us are read in that Z formation, most of us write in a hunt and peck typewriter formation. (For those of you who have seen a typewriter only in a museum, the structure here was to write to the end of the far right of the device, whereupon manually or electrically, the carriage would loudly return, breaking the concentration and zooming back to the beginning of the next line on the left-hand side. Quite annoying for flow.)

We bury ideas and expect the reader to be able to pick up all the loose ends of things that we have scattered throughout our sentence. Here's where transition can help. By using strong transition between sentences, organization comes riding to the rescue of clarity, and helps you make sure that your ideas are clear.

Think of transition between sentences as a taut chain. A loose chain allows gaps. If you have a chain link bracelet, for example, you'll have spaces between where one link hooks into the other. You'll also have the risk of losing that bracelet as it flops and dangles on your wrist. That may be okay for a bracelet, but let's say that you want to chain your bicycle outside the nearest coffee shop. The looser the chain, and the more open the space between links, the more likely someone can snip through one of the links and your bicycle won't be there when you're ready to leave with your latte.

You want your chain links to be taut and pull on each other; that gives you the greatest strength. Writing is no different; the links need to pull tightly. That means that unlike the typewriter hunt and peck structure, your writing has to be prepared for that reader who reads in the Z formation. In other words, the last word or two of the sentence must tightly cling to the beginning of the next. In that way, the sentence forms a strong chain.

In the previous sentence illustration, we can play in many ways to build stronger clarity and transition depending on what the writer's main idea is.

Let's go back to our sentence:

Thousands of outdoor winter enthusiasts descend upon Aspen every winter.

Ideally, to have flow, you need that taut chain. So your next sentence should refer to winter; because that is your last idea in the sentence, it is the indicator of where the idea is going. So you would write something that looks like this:

Thousands of outdoor winter sports enthusiasts descend upon Aspen every winter. During January and February, the ice carnivals, bonfires, and heavy snowfall create ideal conditions for all sorts of winter sports.

See how *each winter* is tightly connected to *During January and February?*

But what if the writer wants to focus on Aspen, not the winter? To achieve that flow, he has to adjust his transition:

> *Every winter, thousands of outdoor winter enthusiasts descend upon Aspen.*

Now he can talk about Aspen, as in

> *Every winter, thousands of outdoor winter sports enthusiasts descend upon Aspen. The town, built to emulate a European village, contains both affordable and luxurious accommodations and restaurants, which draw tourists from all over the globe.*

The main idea is outdoor winter enthusiasts? Again he has to change transition:

> *Every winter, Aspen plays host to thousands of outdoor winter sports enthusiasts. These skiers, snowboarders, ice skaters, and snowman fanatics congregate in Colorado's premiere resort town.*

And if the main idea is about the thousands? You know what to do by now: adjust the structure to adjust the flow.

> *Every winter, outdoor winter sports enthusiasts descend on Aspen by the thousands—58 percent of the 64.3 million tourists who visited the town in 2016 arrived between December 2015 and March 1, 2016.*

Easy stuff.

Transition Between Paragraphs

If a sentence is an idea, then a paragraph is a group of similar ideas that all fall under the same main idea umbrella. The sentences, therefore, come together to convey one developed idea. And those developed ideas, what we call paragraphs, also have to contain signals to the reader; without those signals, the reader won't know how you see that the ideas relate.

You can use the same transitory devices listed above for transition within paragraphs and to give transition between paragraphs in a longer work. Let's say your first paragraph describes in detail the benefits of a local bakery/coffee shop where you regularly relax and work:

> *The Sunflour bakery has free wifi, plenty of electrical outlets to recharge your devices, and tables that sit slightly lower than standard—perfect for laptop users. One-chair tables circle the window area, which allow those who come to work as well as enjoy and have coffee to be relieved of the guilt of occupying a table meant for two or four. Large and bright lamps hang from the ceiling, providing plenty of light for writing projects or simply checking email. And all this ease is accompanied by the availability of fresh pastries, soups, and breads prepared in the open kitchen behind the counter.*

But the place isn't perfect, which is what you want to describe in detail in the next paragraph. So you use the device that fits your logical need:

> **However**, *working at the Sunflour can be difficult, mainly because it is also a popular place for children.* **Despite** *the relatively high cost of cookies, a steady stream of young children and boisterous teenagers occupies the bakery. And while each one of them seems to be noisy and energetic upon entering the store, once they take a look at the daily offerings, they also become more physical: hopping, dancing, and in some cases climbing up on the display case to get a better look.*

Another strong way to create transitions between paragraphs is to have those good old topic sentences that you were told to create in an outline. If your main idea is that the Polaris 3-D printer is a good acquisition for your firm, then you can give transitions between your paragraphs by topic sentences:

To begin with, having this printer will allow us to create the specialty parts we need to repair the copier instead of having to order them.

Having the printer will also allow us to have greater control over the quality of these parts.

Finally, the printer costs only $5000 and the materials for a year's worth of printing costs only $1000, while ordering parts has cost on average $3240 a year for the past three years.

Transitions keep the reader focused, clear as to where you are leading him. They also help you determine if you are indeed going where you want to go.

Unity and Repetition of Key Words Show You Are on the Right Path

You can also create flow and transition by repeating key words or phrases (and their synonyms). If you are talking about the cost of a particular software, perhaps, you can repeat the name of the software, call it *the software* or *plug-in*, or call it by its name. You can refer to the cost as *expense, expenditure, rate, fee,* or even *price.*

As you use these keywords, however, be aware of all too common disease among writers: it's called *thesaurusitis.* Some of the symptoms include the use of overlong words, half synonyms, and words that just jar against the simplicity of what could be otherwise clear communication. Thesaurusitis happens often when young people head off to college after they have learned many large words to take college entrance exams; if not checked and cured in college, this disease can flare up again as these young people move into a career, wherein they try to be taken seriously. It also attacks people who are more concerned about impressing rather than expressing, which can happen at any age.

This disease often hinders efforts to be both clear and professional. How? For instance, the writer may be talking about a cat. And to vary her words so that she doesn't keep saying cat, she consults with a thesaurus. Used to be we had to buy a book called a thesaurus to find those words that seemed to be replacements for the word we were using; today we have all manners of online, readily available thesauri.

Having these tools so handy can be dangerous, however. Often we succumb to relying on them and not on our own good sense or knowledge of the language. And therefore, we lay ourselves open to catching Thesaurusitis. A thesaurus will give you as your choices for a replacement for *cat* words such as *feline, creature,* and *animal.* But with most thesauri, you will also get words such as *tiger* and *panther.* If you are writing about Fluffy the house cat, these words are inappropriate.

Because most of us know the difference between a tiger, a panther, and the ordinary shorthaired tabby, we don't make the mistake of choosing the inappropriate word. But in a larger context, with words whose definitions we may not be totally sure of, we make many mistakes. To those who do know the difference in words, those mistakes glow in neon. The writer has indeed made an impression, but not one he'd like to have. Your best bet is to find a good dictionary of synonyms that will not only offer replacement words, but their definitions, their connotations, and explanations as to how they should be used. Did you know that a *shriek*, a *scream*, a *holler*, and a *yell* are not interchangeable? A good dictionary of synonym use will make those distinctions clear.

> **Caveat:** To achieve flow, make sure your ideas are arranged correctly. Otherwise you will find yourself wandering and doubling back—and are guaranteed to lose your reader.

While J.R.R. Tolkein's quote admonishes us that "Not all who wander are lost," unfortunately most of us who wander when we write lose everyone else. By establishing the logical relationships between your ideas, you may very well see that the ideas are logically out of order. Noticing that is a good thing: better that you fix it and rearrange the order logically than have your reader think, *"Where in the world is he going with this stuff?"*

Think strategically as well. While you do want your headline up front, do you want your strongest point to also be up front? Logically, no. Once you have grabbed the reader's attention, what you want to do is build a case. And that means that you start with the weakest argument and build to the strongest. Or you can start with the most familiar and build to the most innovative.

In essence, you want your message to capture the audience's attention. Therefore, think about the audience (yes, we're back to that again) and then build the story of your message to keep them interested. How you make your ideas relate logically determines how interested they will be. Take a moment to examine your organization; would you have a stronger logical relationship if you moved a few ideas around?

However, one just can't decide, "Oh, I'll just move the important words that I'm talking about the end of the sentence" and move on. Strong transition requires that you pitch the unnecessary. It requires that you take a good hard look at what's important in your sentences, cut the unneeded, and then arrange so that the chain becomes taut.

In other words, the Zen principle of non-attachment plays a role here.

> While connecting ideas together is not only fun but necessary for your reader or listener to follow your path, you must detach from your own thoughts long enough to see the structure.

A good friend once said that she'd never detached from anything that didn't leave her with long claw marks all over it. But you have to detach to see if the flow is clear. As Hindu Prince Gautama Siddharta, the founder of Buddhism, who lived around 563–483 B.C and whom we refer to as Buddha, is reported to have said,

> *As irrigators lead water where they want, as archers make their arrows straight, as carpenters carve wood, the wise shape their minds.*

Shape your mind to create a clear path. Only then can you offer—or find—enlightenment.

CHAPTER 14

Honor Truth (or What You Don't Know That Can Hurt Your Career)

Don't use words too big for the subject. Don't say infinitely when you mean very; otherwise you'll have no word left when you want to talk about something really infinite.

— C.S. Lewis

The world is full of truths that can help you advance your career—yet often those truths aren't taught in school. They may not have been taught at home, either, if the parents didn't know these truths themselves. Tidbits such as how to have a perfect handshake or how to take a $99 jacket to a tailor to get a fit that makes it look like you spent $1000 are all but lost in the dust of today's large corporations. Yet they still matter.

You can get all the grammar and goals right in your writing but still not convey the written professional polish that you want. Yet unless someone has taught you how to achieve that polish, chances are good you'll never achieve it. That's what this chapter is all about.

Basic Advice No One May Have Ever Told You: Keep It in Plain English

Have you ever heard someone say, "Tell me that again in plain English?" What they're asking for is for you to clarify what you have said. But what is plain English?

Plain English is, in basic terms, close to the spoken English most of us use in our everyday transactions. Technically, linguists say that plain

English is conversational word choice that most people with an 8th grade education can understand. The bad news is that studies such as the nation's report card indicated that only 28 percent of our high school graduates are capable of writing in plain English. So what do we have to do?

Plain English means that you write the way you talk—when you are talking in your clearest and best fashion.

Note that plain English is not talking in your most "educated" fashion. An odd thing happens to people when they think that someone is going to judge their writing or speaking. They move from plain English into what they think they should sound like. As a result, their messages usually become very obtuse. This common phenomenon led to passage of the 2013 Plain Language Act that requires that all U.S. government documents be written in a style that can be read and understood at a first cursory glance.

Plain English does have some limitations. It does not, for instance, express deep emotions or dialect differences. But what it does do is provide a *lingua franca* for business and for general conversation. In the Southern U.S., we may say we are "fixing to" do something, meaning we are about to start something. While that is common plain English in the South, it is not mainstream plain English—and is therefore unacceptable in most professional communications.

Plain English used as a guideline keeps you from sounding pompous, overbearing, or generally clueless. Someone who is educated is someone who can express herself clearly, simply and well, whose message anyone can understand. That way you avoid such monstrosities as "the perpetrator of the misdemeanor was apprehended while absconding with a motorized vehicle in a public place of recreation." Say what? As we discussed in an earlier chapter, if you go back and translate this sentence, what you wind up with is "the thief was caught while stealing a car in the park." Isn't that second one much easier to understand?

Mark Twain's rule of thumb for writers to "never use a quarter word when a nickel word will do" doesn't necessarily mean that one should never use a quarter word. (A quarter word, to Twain, was a word that was three or more syllables.). It meant not to use a big word when a small word would suffice. For instance, why should people try to *facilitate* something when they could say *guide?*

Being clear means being aware of all of the word's meanings.

Remember that words have baggage. They have not only denotations, which is the dictionary definition of what the word means, but connotations. A connotation is the emotional overtone or the level of power that the word carries.

The word *facilitate,* for instance, comes from *facile,* or simple-minded; it means to make things easy for the simple-minded to understand. If I'm going to *facilitate* something, that denotation says I have superior knowledge or superior ability—and implied in that word is a sense, as we noted above, of condescension. But *guide* puts us on equal footing. *Guide* shows that I'm willing to become your partner and that I respect you and your; you just need help, as all of us do at one time or another. The one-syllable word is powerful in its simplicity, respect, positive impact, and of course clarity.

One may argue that in many of today's business and legal documents, we don't see plain English. We see instead large clumps of gobbledygook. That use of gobbledygook is deliberate. Some lawyers and some companies purposely choose to be so obtuse or confusing that they think they are keeping themselves and their clients out of court. However, an increasingly number of lawyers are finding plain English works better. Citibank, for instance, discovered after introducing a plain English promissory note that the number of collection lawsuits fell dramatically. Writing clearer instructions and details allowed those who were signing the promissory notes to understand what they were signing—and allowed them to keep their promise better.

This whole idea takes us back to what we have started with: how can I communicate if I don't know what you mean and you don't know what I mean? Communication is an agreement, a bond between two or more people, to share ideas. If we try to hide our ideas behind big words or a lot of verbiage, we don't create that bond. A lack of plain language always catches up with you.

Keep It Parallel

Another way to give structure to your communication is to use parallel construction. Doing so is one of the simplest ways to add clarity to your writing. Based on the concept of parallel lines, this technique organizes your thoughts so that the reader can understand quickly and easily what you mean.

In math, two lines are considered parallel when they follow the same plane; that means that if you plot them on a graph, they never intersect. When one builds a building, for example, one uses parallel structure. Think about it; if you didn't have two parallel posts, putting a roof on the building would be very hard to do. You may see some buildings where you do have slanted roofs or vaulted ceilings, but what holds them up is parallel. Even nature arranges things in parallel construction. Trees will grow in parallel form unless conditions and man and weather change those conditions.

Convinced? Let's explore how you can make your writing parallel. First you have to understand what we mean we talk about the *construction of a sentence*. Basically, the construction of a sentence means how you build it. It means how you arrange the parts. Is your noun first? Or is the verb first, as in the way you would build a question? Let's say that you have a couple of items that need to go together, such as items in a series or a list. To remain parallel, the structure of the first item determines the structure of the following items.

Parallel structure means that you build all of your related ideas in the same manner.

For example, look at the following sentence:

In order to increase our productivity, we need to buy some new software, invest in training, and we really need to hire some more people.

Read that sentence aloud. Do you hear how even though that last idea is sort of clear, it seems to jar and be disjointed and fuzzy? That's because it's not parallel. We started the first of the three items with a very simple construction, as in *buy some new software*. We started with a verb and ended with the direct object of that verb. (Remember that the direct object answers the question *what?* immediately after the verb. In this case you're answering *buy what?*).

The second item you have is *invest in some training*. *Invest* is your verb; *training* is your direct object. Here these two items are parallel. They both start with a verb and they both end with a direct object. We have built them in the same construction. Now look at that third one: *We really need to hire some more people*. Well, we have a verb, but it comes after a noun. Did we have a noun in the first two? We did not. By starting with that pronoun we have broken parallel construction.

Human minds take in words that are written in parallel construction much more easily than they take in words that are written and nonparallel construction. And fixing nonparallel is very simple. The easiest way to fix this error is to look at how we built the first phrase, then make the second one match. In this case, all we need to do is cut the pronoun *we* in the phrase as well as cut the adverb *really*. *We* don't have an adverb in the first two, so we can't have an adverb in the third one. Now we are left with the verb *hire*. So our third item now becomes *hire some more people*.

Let's look at the revised sentence:

To increase our efficiency, we need to buy some new software, invest in some training, and hire some new people.

The idea is the same, but by putting it in parallel construction we have made the idea easier to follow. We've made it easier for the reader to comprehend.

Watch the Emphasis

Another way to use sentence construction for clarity lies in the concept of emphasis. You can read a simple sentence such as "John told me to go to the store" in a variety of different ways, each of which gives the sentence a different meaning. You could emphasize the word *John*, indicating that it's important that John told you to go to the store. You could also emphasize *me*, which means you are telling the reader that it is important that you were the one who went to the store. Or you could emphasize *told*, which gives an impression that some sort of friction is going on in the situation in which the sentence was spoken. Each varying placement of emphasis gives a whole different meaning to how the audience receives the message.

While we usually think of this emphasis as something that is spoken, you can use emphasis in writing as well. You don't have to italicize a word in order to get its emphasis across. Using emphasis in writing is far deeper than that—but it isn't any harder.

In writing emphasis, the sentence flows in a manner that creates a definite path. That path from one idea to the next makes the next idea connect so that it emphasizes the words you want emphasized.

To create the emphasis path, all you need are the rules—and they are simple. For instance a good sentence, like a good paragraph, is the opposite of a sandwich. In the sandwich, what is in the middle is what is important. You don't go around saying, "I'm going to have a whole wheat sandwich today." Instead, you say, "I'm going to have a BLT." The important part is the middle of the two pieces of bread, or what you are going to have. That's the first rule of the sandwich.

But in a sentence or in a paragraph, what's in the middle is seen as not important. Most of us just skip right over what is in the middle. Only the beginning and middle register. So let's look at the following sentence:

Each winter many people go to Colorado to ski.

Depending on how we structure the sentence, we send a message of what is important in that sentence. Take a look: in the sentence as it is written: the word *Colorado* is in the middle of the sentence. Because we skip right over the middle words, the word *Colorado* most likely won't register as a concrete idea in our minds.

If, however, *Colorado* is the important word to the meaning we want to convey, we need to move it around. Observe: because people pay attention to the beginning, we know that their mind is caught by the idea of *each winter*. But then, by the construction of the sentence, we throw the idea of *winter* away and move on to other things. If we want the main idea of what we are talking about to focus on *winter*, we need to move it around.

Since we also know that people pay attention to what goes at the end of the sentence, we know that their mind is caught by the idea of *skiing*. The end, by the way, is known as the sweet spot, the part of the sentence that most people pay the most attention to. They do so simply because it is the end. Human minds are like that; instead of enjoying each piece in the journey, we can hardly wait to get to the end. So whatever word we put at the end of the sentence takes on greater importance. If we know that the word *Colorado* is what we want the reader to pay attention to, we need to move it to the end of the sentence.

How do you know whether to move it around? Or where to move it to? That's where the rules of sentence emphasis come in:

Rule 1: What lies in the middle of the sentence isn't important.
Rule 2: What comes first catches the reader's attention.
Rule 3: The reader will forget what caught his attention by the time he gets to the end of the sentence. So don't pick up the idea from the first part of the sentence in the following sentence; the reader will be confused.
Rule 4: The words at the end of the sentence usually are the ones the reader remembers the most.

So let's go back to previous sentence. If the idea of *winter* is what the next sentence is going to be about, we need to move it to the end. Therefore, we now have:

Colorado is the destination for many skiers each winter.

We replaced the word *Colorado* in the middle with the word *destination*; it's a throwaway word that we really don't need except for making the sentence grammatically correct. What the reader comes away with, however, is that *Colorado* is the *winter* place to be if you are a skier, which is what we really want to convey in the sentence. We can also say:

Many skiers head to Colorado each winter.

In this form, we place *Colorado* in the background, catching the idea with a focus on skiers and then building up steam with the idea of *each winter*. We can also turn the sentences around even more; we can say:

Each winter skiers flock to Colorado.

By putting *Colorado* at the end of the sentence, we give it emphasis. We place the emphasis we want in the reader's mind. And the idea is taut and clear. Without a taut and clear idea chain, you wind up with a loose lump of junk. Observe:

Many skiers head to Colorado each winter. These skiers are drawn by the lure of the Rockies and deep snow.

Do you hear how the reader has to head all the way back to the start of the previous sentence to continue the idea? Do you see how the chain is loose? The sentence, in fact, is so loose that the second sentence has to almost repeat the first one to build the idea. Sentence construction such as this one slows down the reader. He has to mentally go back several times, recalling and repeating ideas in his head even if the ideas aren't repeated on the page. The reader forms an unconscious opinion that the person who wrote the sentence isn't someone whose work is pleasant to read, even if the ideas in the writing are quite good.

The two-steps-forward-one-step-back construction is almost as bad. Take a look:

Many skiers head to Colorado each winter. The state has many different types of ski resorts, all with the lure of the Rockies and deep snow.

Here the reader doesn't have to go back as far, so the chain is a little tighter than the first version. But the construction of the sentence slows everything down more than necessary. What would we do to make the sentence tight? Depends on what we want to emphasize and where we want to go next with the ideas:

> *Many skiers head to Colorado each winter. The deep snow, coupled with high slopes and icy majesty of the Rockies, makes the state a skiers' paradise. Luxurious accommodations and a variety of non-skiing winter sports are almost impossible for serious skiers to resist.*

or

> *Each winter, many skiers head to Colorado. But the state has much to offer in the summer as well. During June, the Rockies come alive with wild flowers; in July, rodeos and fly fishing abound.*

Do you see how the word order creates the path to emphasis?

In Zen, when you set off in a destination, you must consider carefully what path you want the reader to take.

As a writer, you have to have both a clear path and a clear destination for your reader. Without it, your reader will wander.

Remember the conversation between Alice and the Caterpillar in *Alice in Wonderland*?

> "Would you tell me, please, which way I ought to go from here?"
>
> *"That depends a good deal on where you want to get to."*
>
> *"I don't much care where—"*
>
> *"Then it doesn't matter which way you go."*

Emphasis is easy when you know where you want to go. Deciding that, however, may be the hardest part.

Say Bye-Bye to By

The word *by* is a preposition. Prepositions, you may recall, are small words that connect larger and more important parts of speech—which means that the preposition connects more important ideas. Although prepositions have their place, that place is never important, and never ever important enough to be the subject of a sentence.

> You will never have a preposition as your subject for the sentence.

Therefore, you will never have *by* in the subject. Just think logically: a preposition is a preposition, and it isn't a noun. Even when it dresses itself up as a prepositional phrase, it isn't a noun, no matter how hard it may pretend to be one. If you try to make a preposition your subject, you will wind up with a mess of muddy communication that still needs a subject. Look, for example, at the following:

By communicating effectively with your employees, it helps lift morale.

If you look carefully, you will see that you have that indefinite *it.* You added that pronoun, weak and unclear as it is, to try to have a subject. But does the reader or listener truly know what you are talking about? No. This sentence lacks clarity. (Amazing how all these concepts intertwine, isn't it?)

So how do you fix this mess?

Simple: Cut the *by.* And then cut the noun or pronoun you inserted because of the *by.*

By communicating effectively with your employees, it helps lift morale
becomes

Communicating effectively with your employees helps lift morale.

Hacking away at verbosity and clutter that *by* brings will increase your image substantially.

Being. . . .

Starting a sentence with the words *being as* or *being that* is a recipe for a pompous, unclear sentence. These are unnecessary starters designed to focus attention on the writer and not on the message of the sentence. You want your message to speak for you, not your self-importance. Consider this sentence:

Being that I am an English major, I have to spend a lot of time reading.

Such wording indicates that you really want the receiver to see you, the writer, rather than the message. To fix it, replace the *being that* with *since*. You can even cut further:

As an English major, I have to spend a lot of time reading.

Being as it is that we are meeting Friday, let's cancel Thursday's meeting.

now becomes

Since we're meeting Friday, let's cancel Thursday's meeting.

Much better.

And the Ones I Hope You Know. . .

In business, communication should look like business. It shouldn't look like a teenaged mall rat who wants to be cool. If your Great Aunt Maude wouldn't understand your words, then write it in words that she would understand. Don't use text shortcuts or text language in a business communication.

Texting is still communicating, and you need to adapt to your audience. If you want to text your BFF, it may be OK to write *C u l8r.* If you have an appropriate opportunity to text a colleague or your boss, write *See you at the meeting tomorrow.* Your image is at stake.

Also, use correct capitalization. While e.e. cummings could get away with writing with no capital letters, for anyone else, it is an affectation. You can have your freedom of speech—just know that your employer has the same freedom to fire you if your speech puts the organization in a bad light.

To Sum Up

These points are small. Yet they are all vital points. In professionalism as in writing—and in life—details make all the difference.

CHAPTER 15

Know the Devil in the Details

You must remember, Madame Harris, elegance is in the details.
—Lynn Sheene, *The Last Time I Saw Paris*

Ever see a man dressed in what should be the ultimate of business professional wear, yet somehow he just doesn't look right? Or a woman who should send the image of a competent careerist, but who comes across instead as a wannabe?

Those who know can tell you what's wrong: perhaps the lapels on the man's jacket are too wide, his pants an inch too long, her shoes inappropriate to the outfit, or the skirt sagging a bit in back. These details are often the devil to get right, yet like the proverbial icing on the cake, they determine whether the efforts succeed or not.

Much the same occurs in your business communication. You can get the 5 W's right and have a dead-eye aim for your audience, but if the details are wrong, your image sinks. You can have a great Italian suit, handmade shoes, great tone, and as much charm as the day is long. Yet you can blow your polished image with any of these tricky little errors.

Applying the ideas in this chapter will help ensure that your communication prospers:

Make Sure Your Subjects and Verbs Agree

This concept, one of the first we learn in elementary school, can be one that we feel so confident about that we miss agreement errors without realizing it. Most of us won't write *The cat are on the ledge*, but we may write *millions of barrels of oil was highjacked* and not blink an eye. What happens here is that we see the noun closest to the verb, make the verb agree with it, and move on.

Yet the noun closest to the verb is often not the subject. Look at the sentence above; it contains two prepositional phrases, *of barrels* and *of oil*. The subject is actually *millions*. So do you write *millions was highjacked?* You wouldn't if those prepositional phrases weren't in the way. But here you need them, and without a careful eye, you can overlook the error. Be aware of those prep phrases, especially the ones that start with *of*. Your subject will never be in a prep phrase; the noun in those is called the *object of the preposition*—which is probably more than you want to know about grammar. To check yourself, just go to the tool bar in your document, click on "find," and then type in "of." Then look carefully; is the "of" phrase in the way of your agreement?

Keep Your Related Parts of the Sentence Together

Another way to ensure that your subjects and verbs agree is to keep the parts of the idea together. Look at the sentence below:

> *Rodriguez, in a tied game at the bottom of the ninth with the bases loaded and a chance of a winning run on third, struck out.*

Here you have so much junk between the subject and the verb that by the time you get to the verb, you've forgotten who you're talking about. Simply moving the subject next to the verb clears up the sentence:

> *In a tied game at the bottom of the ninth with the bases loaded and a chance of a winning run on third, Rodriguez struck out.*

Did you notice, by the way, that the issue in this sentence was clouded by the same issue in the *millions of barrels of oil* sentence? Those pesky prep phrases are at work again, which leads to the next rule.

Don't Let Your Modifiers Dangle

Quick: What's wrong with this sentence?

When thinking about online harassment, cyber-bullying of children is often a topic of conversation.

Who's doing the thinking? The writer apparently meant *we* or *I*, but the way this sentence is structured implies that the cyber-bullying is doing the thinking. Any modifier—word, phrase, or clause that describes—that starts a sentence must refer to the subject of the sentence. And here cyber-bullying is the subject.

These dangling modifiers usually occur when the writer is trying to remove himself from the document, or at least remove the first person reference. Yet by doing so he creates another gaffe—one that many others will notice immediately.

The usual fix to a dangling modifier is to ask who is doing the action that describes. So fixing *While singing to my new baby, the dog began to howl* is easy—*While I sang to my new baby the dog began to howl.* However, removing the first-person reference in the cyber-bullying sentence requires a little more work. You can fix this sentence in a number of ways. You can say

Thoughts of online harassment lead to the topic of cyber-bullying of children.

Or you can say

Cyber-bullying of children is an especially recognizable form of online harassment.

The key is to slow down and ask yourself what you really mean. Doing so usually creates a much better sentence.

Fix Redundancies

Redundancies come about when we are thinking one thing and communicating another. As a result, we wind up saying the same thing twice—or more. The message repetitions send isn't that we are being careful; it's that we aren't paying attention to our own thoughts.

Some common redundancies and how to fix them

absolutely certain	*Certain* means absolute. This redundancy sounds typical of a teen-aged girl, which isn't the image you want.
the honest fact/the honest truth	Facts and truths are supposed to be absolute. By adding the *honest* you send signals that maybe perhaps you've taken liberties with other facts and truth.
add an additional	If you are adding it, it is additional. Use *in addition* instead.
advance planning/plan ahead	Planning means to do in advance or ahead.
end result/final outcome	Result or outcome is the end, and it's final. Just cut the first term.
group meeting	A meeting is usually comprised of a group of people. If you're meeting just with one person, then label it a *one-on-one meeting* or *conversation*.
assemble together	Because *assemble* means "to put together," just use *assemble*.
careful scrutiny	*Scrutiny* means to look at something carefully; just cut the adjective here.
cooperate together	*Cooperating* means to work together.

Avoid Poor Constructions

Faulty constructions occur when we aren't sure what we are saying, so we put around a bit before getting to business. They can undermine the most effective statements, simply because they send the message that we're unsure of our own thoughts and have begun to communicate before we are sure what we want the receiver to understand. Take a look:

Some faulty constructions and how to fix them

In the report, it states. . .	Cut the prep phrase and the pronoun. Just say, "*The report states. . .*"
This email is going to explain. . .	Why not just do it? Your audience will follow you faster if you give the explanation with no warmup.
I would like to thank you. . .	So what is stopping you? Just do it: *Thank you for the time you spent last week showing me how to work the new copier.*
and/or	This convenient shortcut will get you in trouble every time. Consider the case of a hospital emergency room in an inner city area, whose policy stated: "*Physicians must get background on patient's medical history and/or whether a family member has had the same issue.*" Over 50 percent of the ER cases were shootings, knifings, and drug overdoses, yet the physicians, wanting to abide by policy and confused by the and/or, dutifully asked even these patients if they had a family member with the same issue. The docs lost a great deal of time filling in the paperwork for those answers, not to mention the hospital lost a lot of neighborhood respect for being seen as "nosy."

Wipe Out the Down and Dirty Errors

Seemingly small oversights in your writing can cause significant negative impressions among your readers. Watch out for the following writing foibles.

Sentence fragments

Fragments are snatches of ideas, caused by the writer's not checking to see if she has both a subject and a fully functioning verb in the sentence. Often writers are tricked into thinking they have both of these necessary parts; being aware of a few of the main tricksters is helpful.

Starting a sentence with an adverb. Remember the old saw about putting the cart before the horse? That's what often happens when you start a sentence with an adverb; your thoughts get ahead of themselves and create confusion. If you take any complete sentence and add an adverb in front of it, you demote the sentence to be a partial thought. Look at the sentences below.

> *How a manager can improve his team's performance without demoralizing punishment.*

Here the writer intends to tell how. But he's so focused about telling us how that he's hidden the what. A revised version would look something like this:

> *A manager can improve his team's performance without demoralizing punishment.*
>
> *Here's how.*

Check your adverbs. Use the handy "find" feature in your tool bar and plug in standard adverbs such as *how, when,* and *where.* Check your sentences. If you find yourself in the adverb-first muddle, clean it up.

Starting a sentence with a subordinator. Closely aligned with the adverb-first error, this one also demotes a full idea. In this error, the writer's thoughts lag behind him; he's thinking about how the ideas connect to previous ideas, but not clearly indicating that connection to the reader.

> *Because the manager used Kotter's principles of change.*

What happened because the manager used these change principles? The writer doesn't tell us. He's set up a cause-and-effect situation, but neglected to tell us the effect. A revision would look something like the following:

Because the manager used Kotter's principles of change, the team was able to transition to the new expectations with very few resignations or firings.

Starting a sentence with an infinitive. This error also usually occurs because the writer isn't thinking in the moment. She loses focus of what the sentence is supposed to be saying, as shown in the following example:

To think that the strategy will make a difference for the employee's understanding of the organization.

What she's done here is lose her way; she's thinking about the strategy's effect, or at least thinking that someone else should be thinking about it, but wandering away from the idea's direct path. A revision may look like the following:

The strategy will make a difference for the employee's understanding of the organization.

or

The manager's approach to the strategy will make a difference for the employee's understanding of the organization.

Starting a sentence with a participle. Sometimes writers think that a word that ends in *ing* is a full verb. It isn't. It is a participle, or part of the verb. Therefore, it needs a helping verb to be a full verb. But being unaware of that need creates fragments, as in the following:

The employees getting the work done in a timely manner.

With just the participle here, what the writer intends to be the verb becomes a descriptor, or a phrase that describes the subject. What about these employees? If the answer is just that they are getting the work done, add the helping verb:

The employees are getting the work done in a timely manner.

But if the results are something else, then add that full verb to your sentence:

The employees getting the work done in a timely manner has helped our bottom line.

Verbs matter. Find the verb in each sentence, make sure it truly is a verb, and then make sure it has a subject that it pairs with.

Mistaking a verb in a phrase as your main verb. Consider the following:

The value of what the worker has done thus far.

Note here that the writer sees *has done* and thinks he has a verb. Well, she does, but the verb is part of the phrase that begins with *of what.* The *of* demotes the phrase away from being either a main subject or verb, so the main subject, *the value,* is left with no action. It is therefore a fragment and tells the reader nothing. To fix these errors, keep a list of common prepositional phrases handy and again employ the "find" feature in your tool bar. Then ask yourself what you want to say about the part of the sentence you do have. A revised version of this sentence would ask, "What about the value?" The answer would then yield a sentence that may look like the following:

The manager has to value the efforts that the worker has made thus far.

Writing with too many prepositional phrases. This error often occurs because the writer hasn't totally formulated his thought. Preposition phrases are parts of ideas, not full ideas. Yet often writers feel that string-ing a bunch of them together creates a full thought. Observe:

> *The ability to grow and to overcome issues with the current employees by use of creative leadership.*

If we slow down and separate out all the different prepositional phrases, we have the following:

- *to grow*
- *to overcome issues*
- *with the current employees*
- *by use*
- *of creative leadership*

And what are we left with? *The ability* and a random *and*. Not a full sen-tence. To fix the error, ask yourself what you want to say about the words that are left, as here you would ask "what about the ability?" The answer will give you the revised and corrected sentence:

> *The ability to grow and to overcome issues with the current employees by use of creative leadership will save the company money by reducing turnover.*

Prepositions are legitimate parts of speech. Prep phrases, which begin with a preposition and end with a noun, are also legitimate; they can add details that clarify a sentence. But while they are valid, they are like per-fume: a little is nice while too much stinks. Check to see what you really intend those prep phrases to do; are you asking them to describe, as in *The man with the red hair argued with the receptionist?* Here you are asking that phrase to describe, which is an adjective's job. So use the adjective: *The red-haired man argued with the receptionist.*

You're not going to be able to cut all prep phrases; checking to see which ones you can, however, can lead to stronger sentences.

Word misuse. Words that sound alike or are spelled nearly alike can cause confusion for writers. Be careful to use the following words correctly.

Commonly confused word pairs and how distinguish them

to/too	*To* with one *o* is a preposition, as in *to the store*. *Too* with two o's means *also* or *intensely*, as in *I want to go too* or *he is too funny*. Think of the difference in terms of the *o*'s; if you need more, as in *also* or *more intense*, then you need the form with the extra *o*.
then/than	*Then* is time. *Than* is comparison. For example, *We then met for lunch to discuss why Sam made more money than I did on the sale*.
moral/morale	*Moral* is an ethical behavior standard, as in *moral decision*. It indicates one's character. *Morale* means one's emotional state, as in *employee morale*. Think of that e as standing for *emotion* and you will get these two right every time.
affect/effect	This one is tricky. In general, *affect* is a verb while *effect* is the result of that verb (a noun). *Affect* means to have impact on. *Effect* is the result of that impact. Think *a for action*; then realize that you have to have the action before you can have the result of that action. Yet in health care, a patient's *affect* refers to his demeanor. This term came about from doctors discussing the results of either treatment or disease—how the patient had been *affected*. Yet the term became the patient's *affect* and remains that way. You can also use *effect* as a verb meaning to achieve, as in *the new board members effected change*. However, in general, stick with the *a for action/e result of action* rule.
manager/manger	For years I thought this confusion was simply a result of overreliance on spellcheck. However, in recent months several notable publications have used these words incorrectly, so the difference needs to be addressed. A *manger* is a box for large animal feed, as in *Jesus was placed in a manger*. A *manager* is a person.
passed/past	If time has passed since an event happened, it is now in the past. But the word *passed* is a verb. If you mean a thing, as in *before now*, use *past*. That way you refer to the *past tense*, not the *passed tense*.
principle/principal	A *principle* is a rule. Look at the endings of the words *principle* and *rule*: they both end in –le. That's a good tip to help you remember how to use the word. A *principal*, however, is the head or main thing, as in the *principal* reason you've made a decision or the *principal* amount of money you started with in your investment. A *principle* of a school, for instance, is one of the guiding rules, while the *principal* is the person who runs the school. (Think *the principal is my pal* to help you remember—again look at the endings of the two words.)
ensure/insure	The first one means "to make sure of" while the second one means to secure financial value. You *ensure* that someone has paid to *insure* your car.

bias/biased	The first form is a noun. The second one describes. So if you have found bias in an argument, that person who put forth that argument could be considered *biased*.
I/me	Most of us know that we don't write *Me and Tommy went to the store*, at least not in business. The more common mistake in business communication comes when the pronoun comes after *and*. Observe: -*Get the details to Jane and I before the close of day.* -*Come have lunch with my boss and I tomorrow.* I could tell you to learn the difference between subjective pronouns and objective pronouns. But the easiest way to know if you are using the right form is to drop the *so-and-so and* part. Get the details to I? Hardly. Come have lunch with I? No way.
he/him, she/her, they/them, who/whom	The rules for I/me work here as well.

Punctuation misuse. Many writers have problems with the following types of punctuation errors.

- *Apostrophe misuses*—as in the following:

The managers to-do item was to meet with the other manager's.

This one really has no excuse—except that perhaps so few people have explicitly been chastised for misusing an apostrophe. But don't let that lack of overt criticism fool you; those who know the difference in usage will see an apostrophe mistake and automatically, if not consciously, mark you as someone not quite ready for prime time in their corporation.

First, you use an apostrophe and then an s to make a singular noun possessive. So if the bone belongs to a dog, you now write *the dog's bone*. You never use an apostrophe to make a noun plural. If you have more than one dog and they share the bone, you have *the dogs' bone*; when the dog has more than one bone, you now have *the dog's bones*.

About 10 percent of English words make their plurals with internal changes; you just have to be aware of those. So more than one mouse becomes *mice*. But some words have unusual changes for the plural: one moose, for instance, remains *moose* if he is joined by a friend. If the noun ends in the letter *s*, usually you use *es* to make it plural, as in *class* becoming *classes*.

But you never use an apostrophe to make a plural. For a while in the late 1950s and early 1960s, a great to-do and confusion erupted when some grammarians began to argue that if a word ended in *s,* you didn't need to use the *s* after the apostrophe. This gave rise to awkward constructions such as *Prince Charles' grandchildren.* Why are these awkward? Try saying them. You can't say the extra *s* as you would in *Prince William's children.* So by the end of the 1960s most grammarians followed the lead of E.B. White, who wrote

Many a tame sentence of description or exposition can be made lively and emphatic by substituting a transitive in the active voice (p.18).

Yet many people were taught during that confusing deviation era, or were taught by those who were taught during that time, and they have difficulty moving back to mainstream. So if using the *'s* bothers you when you have a possessive noun that ends in *s,* you have an option. You can use a prepositional phrase, as in *the grandchildren of Prince Charles.* Your passage will be readable, you ease your own discomfort, and you are grammatically correct.

Now what about if you are talking about a family whose last name ends in *s?* Well, if you have Ted and Sue Williams, their last name is a noun that ends in *s.* So to make it plural, as occurs when you are talking about the two of them, you write *the Williamses.* You still follow the rule of making a noun that ends in *s* plural by adding *es.* You can also write their name as an adjective, as in *the Williams family.* But if you are talking about their dog, and it belongs to all of them, you first have to make the noun plural and then you add the apostrophe. So you now have *the Williamses' dog.*

You can also use an apostrophe to indicate that you have left out letters to form a contraction, or a shortened form of the word construction. Therefore, *cannot* becomes *can't* and *wouldn't* becomes *won't.* Note that nothing is wrong with using contractions in business communication; in fact, *not* using them makes your communication come across as stiff or too formal. Save these full-out versions for the very rare times you want strong emphasis, as in *I simply cannot allow this unethical behavior to continue.*

- ***Its/it's* confusion.** Closely related to the apostrophe mistake is the using of *its* when you mean *it's*. *It's* always means *it is*, because the writer has contracted the two words. *Its*, however, indicates possession, as in something belonging to it. The easiest way to remember the difference is to understand we are talking about possessive pronouns here. And no possessive pronoun ever has an apostrophe. You don't write *m'y dog* or *hi's job*, do you? So don't write *it's* when you mean possessive.
- ***Comma errors.*** People seem to be confused more about commas than they are about almost anything else in writing. Some never use commas. Some throw them in any old place they think it looks nice. Yet these well-intended efforts always look gauche. The misused comma always glares and stands out—and not nicely, either. Knowing how to use a comma correctly gives you a professionalism and panache. Readers won't stop and say, "hey, she used the comma correctly!" But they will notice your message, not the misplaced comma.

Many people misguidedly believe that a comma needs to be inserted "whenever you pause." No. Let's get this rule straight: you use a comma whenever the idea pauses. You could be one of those who talk forever and never take a breath—and hence have no commas. (Just so you know if you are one of these folks: your speech is most likely as exhausting to listen to as your no-comma prose is to read.) Or you could have the tendency to meander and take many side trips or pauses, most of which are unnecessary. You'll have far too many commas. And your writing will be difficult to follow. See how that "where you pause" mistake detracts from your message?

The easiest way to learn how robust a comma can be that is correctly used is to learn where an idea doesn't pause. An idea has to have a subject and verb—both of them, not just one. An idea never pauses between a subject and verb, between two complete ideas not joined by a conjunction, or between parts of a word grouping. You don't even need to know grammar to scan to see if you have violated that rule. Take a look at this sentence:

The supervisor of our department, argued that we needed stronger safety policies.

Does the idea pause where that comma is placed? No. Is "supervisor of our department" a complete idea? Nope. Is "argued that we needed stronger safety policies" a complete idea? No again. Therefore the comma is misplaced. This sentence needs no comma. If I add a second complete idea, would this use of a comma be correct?

The supervisor of our department argued that we needed stronger safety policies, he has a background with OSHA inspections.

No. Why? Because we have two separate ideas. A comma pauses an idea. But if you have two ideas, you don't have an idea. You have two. And a comma never goes between two complete ideas. These need stronger punctuation or possibly a conjunction to keep those ideas separate. Note that a complete idea never starts with a subordinator. Those are words such as *if, because, when, since,* and *while*. Adding those words to any complete idea subordinates them, or makes them less than complete.

How about the comma use in this one?

The supervisor, of our department argued that we needed stronger safety policies.

No again. The word group includes the prepositional phrase "of our department." You need that phrase to know which supervisor. And you never put a comma in the middle of a word grouping. See? These three "never use" guidelines will work every time.

To add to your arsenal is a should-use rule: if one idea interrupts another and interjects itself before the first idea has finished, set the interrupter off by putting a comma immediately before the interrupter and immediately after it. Doing so indicates that the first idea hasn't finished. So if we change up the sentence in the following manner, do we need the commas?

> *The supervisor of our department, who used to work for OSHA, argued that we needed stronger safety policies.*

We do. The "who used to work for OSHA," while important, interrupts the main idea. So you set it off in commas. Think of the commas as indicating where you can put your hands to lift that interrupter out. (Note that in the first sentence of this paragraph we used this exact technique.)

If you are using a state's name after a city's name in a sentence, the state interrupts. So it goes in commas. If you are using a year in addition to a month and day in a sentence, the year interrupts. So it goes in commas.

> *We moved to Boise, Idaho, when I was three.*

> *Hurricane Hugo hit Charlotte, North Carolina, on September 21, 1989, early that morning.*

One more rule and you're golden: if a subordinated idea comes before a complete idea, put a comma after the end of the subordinated idea. That way you indicate where the lesser gets out of the way of the complete idea—not quite interrupts but does get in the way:

> *Because he had worked for OSHA, the supervisor of our department argued that we needed stronger safety policies.*

If the subordinating idea comes after the complete idea, no comma. It didn't get in the way.

The supervisor of our department argued that we needed stronger safety policies because he had worked for OSHA.

Get your commas right and let the elegance of your punctuation add gloss to your image.

- ### Colon and semicolon misuses
  Quick: see that mark in the middle of a sentence that looks like two dots? And that one that looks like a comma with a dot over it? What are they, and why are they there? You may recognize them as a colon or semicolon, but what exactly do they mean to the message?
  In Zen everything has a purpose. Semicolons and colons are no different. Like all marks of punctuation, semicolons and colons exist not to make your life miserable but to indicate to the reader how to interpret your message. Learning to use semicolons and colons correctly adds subtle but definite power to your communication.
  First, know what they are not. A colon, for instance, does not mean you can forget creating a full idea because you want to add a list. And a semicolon isn't a fancier comma.
  A colon, that erstwhile two dot symbol, means something more is coming. Think of a colon as a neon sign: it indicates that you are going to clarify or add to the complete idea you just conveyed. You can do so with a list, an explanation, or a quotation. But here's the catch: you can use the colon *only* after you have a *complete idea*. That means you have to have a complete sentence before you use the colon. For example, look at this sentence:

To fill in your W9 form you will need: your name, Social Security number, and other personal information.

  Here we have an incorrect use of a colon. Why? Take a look at what comes before that colon. Do we have a complete idea? No. Therefore we can't use the colon. We can use the list of three items, but we don't need the colon. We can just write us a regular sentence with the three items. But if you write the sentence this way:

To fill in your W9 form, you will need the following information: your name, your birthdate, your Social Security number, and other personal information

The colon is right. Why? Because we have a complete idea before that colon. Take a look at these other examples:

Despite all that he did for American foreign policy, most people remember Richard Nixon for only two things: Watergate and his "I am not a crook" speech.

The colon works here because the words that come before it create a complete sentence. You could, however, write that sentence without the colon:

Despite all that he did for American foreign-policy, most people remember Richard Nixon only for Watergate and his "I am not a crook" speech.

In the latter, the two items complete the full sentence so you don't need the colon. To understand how a colon works with a direct quote, look at the difference here:

Lord Rothschild gave this financial advice: "when there is blood in the streets, buy!"

Lord Rothschild gave this financial advice when he said, "when there is blood in the streets, buy!"

And last but not least, remember that a business letter requires a colon after the greeting, not a comma.

A *semicolon*—the one with the comma on bottom and dot on the top— also separates two independent clauses. It's used between two closely related ideas. But here's the catch: the relationship has to be broader than that implied by a conjunction. A conjunction limits the relationship. So an *and* means the two clauses just get added together to make one idea, while a *but* means they contradict each other. If the first clause is the result of the second, use the conjunction *for*; if the second is a result of the first, use *so*. Often, however, the two clauses relate to make one idea, but the relationship isn't as clearly cut as it is with the conjunction. That's when you use the semicolon. For example, look at this sentence:

> *Sam wanted to be Darth Vader for Halloween; his sister saw him more as Yoda.*

Implied here is not direct conflict. Instead, the writer implies that many other factors existed as to why the sister had the opinion she did. You can also use a semicolon between items in a series if one of more of those items has internal punctuation. Look at this example:

The best meal I ever had included an appetizer, which was composed of heirloom tomatoes and handmade mozzarella with dried figs; spinach pasta with a smoked salmon sauce and capers, topped with lobster; and a chocolate torte, made with six different layers of cake and fruit-infused chocolate ganache.

Imagine reading that sentence without the semicolons. The semicolons help keep your reader on track.

- **Hyphens and dashes**
  Those horizontal lines some people use in their writing are either a hyphen or a dash. They look similar, but are used in very different ways. Knowing how to use them correctly can set you apart as someone who understands the finer details of life. The short one, the one that looks like a subtraction sign, is a hyphen. You use those to join two words to make one term. Examples include *co-chairman* or *self-esteem*. Make sure that when you hyphenate words, you are creating one term. So if you talk about your *six-year-old niece*, the *six-year-old* is one term; you need all three words to make that one term to tell us how old your niece is. But if you write *my niece is six years old*, you're not making one term. You are first telling me she is old, which is the main adjective here. Then you are refining it by

saying she's a certain number of years old. Therefore, you don't have one term but three. No hyphen.

Note here that the words that you joined must be the same part of speech. In the examples above, the words are all nouns. You would not write, for instance, *please follow-up on these details*. Why? Because *follow* is a verb and *up* is an adverb (it adds to the verb). They are not the same parts of speech. Yet if you took those two words and turn them into a noun, you would. You would have something like this: *follow-up will occur on December 30*. Here you took the verb and adverb, turned them into one term that now is not an action but a thing, and made those two words into one noun. So you use a hyphen between them to tell your reader that's what you did.

Many terms in the English language that started out as hyphenated have now become so common that they are just bunched together without the hyphen. These include policeman (but not police officer, which is a sad comment on where our society still is).

Before your eyes cross with you decide never to use a hyphen ever again, take a deep breath and remember one thing. All you have to do is pay close attention to how you are using the term. A hyphen joins. The question is whether the things you were joining are alike enough to get along. That's it.

A dash (the long one), however, separates. You are pushing one idea aside for the other. In fact, thinking about pushing the previous word or words aside can help you decide when to use a dash. Imagine that the idea is going forward in one direction. Suddenly that forward motion is halted because something off to the side is commanding attention. You have to change course to deal with that something off to the side. That's what happens with a dash: your idea has been separated from its original intent by something that changes its direction. Observe:

The graph on the screen illustrates—no, wait; those are last quarter's figures.

Think of using a dash when you need to comment on something you just said, or to set it apart from your original idea.

Another helpful image: In theater, a theatrical aside occurs when an actor breaks character and talks to the audience. He is commenting on what he just said or did. That's a dash. To type a dash, type two hyphens, or type two subtraction marks (--), one after the other. Word processing programs will often convert the two hyphens into one longer symbol. And no, you may not use a dash in place of other punctuation. Doing so does not give you style but rather indicates to your reader that you didn't learn how to punctuate or didn't take the time to do it correctly—that you were a little slapdash. (Pun intended.) Not what you want to convey, is it?

In Summary

Correctness in punctuation, grammar, and word usage is polish, just like a gloss on all your other strong attributes. Keeping a watchful eye on the details as you are writing helps keep the devil at bay.

References

Blake, G., and R.W. Bly. 1991. *The Elements of Business Writing*. New York, NY: MacMillan.

Burke, K. 1945. *A Grammar of Motives*. Berkeley, CA: University of California Press.

Covey, S.R. 1989. *The Seven Habits of Highly Effective People: Restoring the Character Ethic*. New York, NY: Simon & Schuster.

Gilovich, T. 1991. *How We Know What Isn't So: The Fallibility of Human Reason in Everyday Life*. New York, NY: Free Press.

Gladwell, M. 2005. *Blink: The Power of Thinking Without Thinking*. New York, NY: Little, Brown & Company.

Glasee, J. July 13, 2014. "Microsoft's New CEO Needs an Editor." *Monday Note*. http://qz.com/233917/microsoft-ceo-satya-nadella-needs-an-editor/.

Gopnik, A. 2005. *The King in the Window*. New York, NY: Hyperion.

Greenfield, R. July 27, 2015. "Your E-mail Font is Ruining Your Life." *Bloomberg Business*. http://www.bloomberg.com/news/articles/2015-07-27/your-e-mail-font-is-ruining-your-life.

Jacobs, A.J. 2011. "My Outsourced Life." In *The 4-Hour Work Week: Escape 9-5, Live Anywhere, and Join the New Rich*, ed. T. Ferriss. New York, NY: Crown Publishers.

Lamott, A. 1994. *Bird by Bird*. New York, NY: Pantheon.

Langer, E.J. 2014. *Mindfulness: 25th Anniversary Edition*. Boston, MA: Da Capo Lifelong Books.

Levy, B.R., Slade, M.D., Kunkel, S.R., and S.V. Kasl. 2002. "Longevity Increased by Positive Self-Perceptions of Aging." *Journal of Personality and Social Psychology*, 83, no. 2, pp. 261–270. doi: 10.1037//0022-3514.83.2.261.

Lewicki, R., Barry, B., and D. Saunders. 2015. "Collecting Nos". In *Negotiations: Readings, Exercises and Cases*. 7th ed. New York, NY: McGraw Hill.

MacDonald, D.A. January 22, 2015. "How Miss America Changed Citibank, Part I," *American Banker*. http://www.americanbanker.com/bankthink/how-miss-america-changed-citibank-part-i-1072276-1.html.

Markham, A. 2014. *Smart Change*. New York, NY: Penguin.

McKinsey Global Institute. 2012. "The Social Economy: Unlocking Value and Productivity through Social Technologies," *Insights and Publications*. http://www.mckinsey.com/industries/high-tech/our-insights/the-social-economy.

Miller, R.L., G.A. Jentz, and F.B. Cross. 2006. *A Guide to Accompany Business Law and Legal Environment Texts*. Mason, OH: South-Western/Cengage Learning.

Munter, M. 1992. *Guide to Managerial Communication.* Englewood Cliffs, NJ: Prentice-Hall.

National Center for Education Statistics. 2011. The Nation's Report Card: Writing 2011. https://nces.ed.gov/nationsreportcard/pubs/main2011/2012470.asp.

Purvis, K. June 30, 2015. "No, I'm Not Done with My Plate Yet," *The Charlotte Observer.* http://www.charlotteobserver.com/living/food-drink/kathleen-purvis/article25835059.html#!

Quible, Z.K., and F. Griffin. 2007. "Are Writing Deficiencies Creating a Lost Generation of Business Writers?" *Journal of Education for Business,* 83, no. 1, pp.32–36.

Strunk, W., and E.B. White. 2000. *Elements of Style.* 4th ed. Boston, MA: Allyn and Bacon.

Suzuki, S. 1983. *Zen Mind, Beginner's Mind.* New York, NY: Weatherhill.

Tannenbaum, Robert, and W.H. Schmidt. March–April, 1958. "How to Choose a Leadership Pattern." *Harvard Business Review.* https://library.goshen.edu/Reserve/DAES%20OLP/How%20to%20Choose%20a%20Leadership%20Pattern.pdf.

Tugend, A. 2011. *Better by Mistake: The Unexpected Benefits of Being Wrong.* New York, NY: Riverhead Books.

Index